AF429287

From Pain to Purpose

BY: NEREIDA VELAZQUEZ

From Pain to Purpose

Copyright © 2024 Nereida Velazquez

NereidaVelazquez.com
nv@NereidaVelazquez.com
www.imdb.com/nereidavelazquez

Nereida Velazquez

Phoenix Rebirth Innovations, LLC

All rights reserved. Reproduction, storage, or transmission of any part of this book in any form, including electronic, mechanical, photocopy, recording, scanning, or others, is strictly prohibited without prior written permission from the publisher. However, brief quotations for critical reviews or articles are allowed.

All Biblical Scriptures were taken from resources found on https://quod.lib.umich.edu/ website.

Distributed by IngramSpark.

Paperback ISBN: 979-8-218-41603-4

Printed in the United States of America.

10 9 8 7 6 5 4 3 2 1

Dedication

James Reynolds, Jr.
June 25, 1923-January 31, 2024

This book is first dedicated to the cherished memory of Grandad, whose wisdom, kindness, generosity, and love will forever illuminate its pages.

I dedicated this work to my children (Melánie, Jonathan, Aysé and Ayden) for being my inspiration, my reason to never give up hope, and my reminders to continue pushing forward. Also, thanks to all my grandchildren (Ella, JJ, Daniella, Jayla, Don, Neo, Emcric) and future grandchildren for being so healing and giving me purpose.

Foreword

The creative spirit, the power of the imagination, or perhaps a soft breeze that disrupts a fluttering butterfly with unyielding turbulence can inspire a writer to his or her first words. As an award-winning writer on stage and in film, I understand inspiration isn't always enough. Inspiration can excite, entertain, and survive without demand or any requirement of sacrifice or courage.

There is indeed power in the pen and the soul, and when the two become one, an undeniable voice of purpose emerges, and the power to change the world emerges. Perhaps Nereida Velazquez subconsciously manifested this journey from *Pain to Purpose*, but as we all know, a broken heart, a dream deferred, a voice silenced, innocence stolen, and hope stripped of its possibilities can enslave us to fear and denial. Even the adults of all adults can harbor a vulnerable child inside of them, screaming for a place to be heard and seen. A place to be loved and a place to belong.

There was indeed a little girl hidden deep within, desperately crying out to be freed from Nereida's fears of being an outcast, judged, criticized, betrayed, and a failure. They needed to be re-united. They needed to remember, fall in love, and learn to trust one another. They needed to believe in each other and take back the right to be authentically human and fulfilled in this life.

When Nereida approached me years ago, nearly demanding that I be her acting coach, she had no idea this would lead to her journey of truth and purpose. Truth can be the thing we're most afraid of. This journey was not easy. The tears were real, and the fear was often times unbearable, but her courage to push through ultimately prevailed.

A writer's pen carries the dreams and inspiration, but sometimes carries the weight of the writer's soul. "Pain to Purpose" bares the soul of Nereida Velazquez, and in her own words, "I consciously chose to heal my heart and mind to free my soul." This book is more than turning the next page. This is a deep dive into the power of manifestation and of self. It is about believing beyond your traumas and circumstances. This is an unveiling of the purest and most vulnerable parts of the soul and the fearlessness to share and bare it all. Word… for… word. Power to all who share this journey.

Javon Johnson

SAG-AFTRA, AEA

Actor/Writer/Director/Acting Coach/Producer

Foreword

Seldom do you meet and have the privilege to work with someone as determined and focused on realizing their full potential as Nereida Velazquez, who is determined to succeed. She has grown tremendously through extremely challenging circumstances in her life. From being teased and made the "butt" of jokes coming from her siblings and friends at school to becoming a mother in her early teens. She has consciously chosen to focus on forgiveness and the self-actualization of her life's goals. She's a true testament to what growing up under difficult circumstances, learning to overcome, and rising to the top looks like.

From the beginning of the acting coach/actor relationship between Nereida and I continued, I witness her became self-aware, she worked on her mind-set via personal growth and development, healed emotionally, physically, and spiritually, found the light that shines within, and discovered her true purpose in life. I applaud you, Nereida, for creating the best version of yourself. Nereida inspires young single mothers and anyone seeking to become the best version of themselves. Yes, you can realize your dreams and goals. Nereida will show you how!

Mike Pointer, Master Coach

Founder: Master Acting and Personal Development Coach
of "Hey, I Saw Your Commercial!" in Los Angeles, California
Author of The Confidence Course For Actors, Feeling Great!
A Medication and - Free Guide To Mental Health Mastery

Foreword

It has been my pleasure to know Nereida Velazquez since 2018. Our lasting relationship has blossomed into more than a friendship; we now feel like sisters. We have joined at the hip since meeting Nereida on my first independent movie set.

Nereida is a strong woman who loves her family and the Lord. The moment we met, we connected instantly. We share some of the same values for family, goals, and ambitions. Nereida has become one of my best friends. I love talking with her a few times weekly to discuss future endeavors.

Now, you can learn more about this beautiful soul as she pours her heart and soul into her novel. You will be amazed by the passion and commitment that Nereida has endured. You will cry, laugh, and connect with her through her words.

Vickie Adams

Producer, Author & Talent Agent

Table of Content

Day 

Healing The Inner Child

It was a warm, lovely sunny summer day with a clear blue sky. The sun shined so bright I could see the ray's reflections on the ground. I searched Google for the forecast. It was predicted to rain later on in the afternoon. As I walked towards the park, I could hear and see the children playing, running, and jumping off the swings. Some were sliding down the slide, and others were climbing the monkey-bars like cute little monkeys. Even the squirrels were playing and chasing each other, running up the big Oak trees. Red Cardinal birds were singing and chirping. I saw dragonflies and blue butterflies flying all around.

As I was walking closer to the playground, I saw a little girl on the swing. She wore an orange short-sleeved dress with white socks and black Chinese shoes. Her hair was dark brown in two braided ponytails with orange barrettes. She was swinging slowly. The other children seemed to have taken off into the meadow field. I sat on the swing closest to the little girl, I heard her say, "Hmm, I wonder where everyone went. I can't see them."

Me: It seems like they all ran into the field. (She looks over at me.)

Little Girl: Oh, hi there. Can you please push me?

Me: Hi. Of course, I can! Can you swing on your own?

Little Girl: Of course I can! (In a high-pitched voice.) But, could you push me? (I began to push her.) Hey. You wanna know what I can do?

Me: What can you do?

Little Girl: I can write with both hands. And, I can do things with my right hand even though it's easier for me to use my left hand. I can't cut paper with my left hand, though. I'm sad about that part.

Me: Why are you sad?

Little Girl: Because I was born a lefty, and that's a bad thing. They make me use my right hand instead. When I'm writing, they take the pencil out of my hand and put it in my right hand. Same thing happens when I'm eating. My Mami's friend took the spoon out of my hand and put it in my right hand just when I was getting ready to put the spoon in my mouth. I looked at her like she was crazy. I was hungry since I didn't eat my lunch at school. I don't like hotdogs or beans. I'm different from everyone. I'm a misfit. Push me higher.

Me: I don't think you should go higher. This is as high as you go.

Little Girl: Oh, come on. Please, we like it high.

Me: Well, I think that's pretty cool that you can write with both hands. And, who told you that you were a misfit?

Little Girl: I heard a grown-up say it. I was being nosy listening to them talking. Well, I do have a bunch of names.

Me: You do, hugh?

Little Girl: Yup. I get called a lot of different names at home. My older brother says I was adopted. Whatever that means. Or, he says, they found me in the trash can. He's just mean and grumpy. They call me Grilla, mantequilla, llorona, hincha, fundillona and…..

Me: How do you feel when they call you all those names?

Little Girl: MMMMM... Not good. But, I'm used to them now. I don't know what Grilla means, but I know why I get called the other names."

Me: Oh, why do you feel like you know why you're being called those names?

Little Girl: Llorona is because I cry more than the others. Fundillona is because I have a big butt. It's hard to find skirts that fit me at the Salvation Army store. I heard them say because I'm Fundillona, a skirt didn't fit me. I did try to squeeze my butt cheeks in, but it didn't work. I'm scared to go to the bathroom at night alone. Sometimes when I'm sleeping, my Mami comes to my room and carries me to the bathroom. You know what else scares me? Every time we go to church, the bad guys break in. I heard it was one of our neighbors. They think my dad is rich, because he drives a new car. The last time the police came to our home, due to a break-in, they checked the living areas of the house and the basement. The police were getting ready to leave, and my older sister heard footsteps in the attic. When my dad checked the attic, no one was there. As he continued to check the house, he passed the basement door and ran into the bad guy in the stairway. The bad guy ran past Papi. He yelled out, and the bad guy ran out the door and dropped a big knife. My dad ran out after him. He returned to the house with the knife he found on the ground. The police saw all of this happen, but did not catch the bad guy. Papi gave the knife to the policeman. Because of the constant break-ins, I hide my little black piano under my bed. I already knew they would come when we went to church. Now, my Papi is selling the house.

Me: Wow. That's scary and so brave of you to tell me this.

Little Girl: Yea. And, I get in trouble for sucking my thumb.

Me: Well, my youngest daughter is a lefty, and she also sucked her thumb. I tried to get her to stop, because it got infected. She just switched thumbs. Sucking your thumb messes up your teeth.

Little Girl: Cool! So, she's like me. Does she have a lot of names, too?

Me: No, only her nickname. And, sometimes, I call her baby.

Little Girl: Oh well. You're wrong about sucking your thumb and messing up your teeth. (She opens her mouth wide with a cheesy smile.) See, my teeth aren't messed up. They are straight and clean. I brush them every day with no cavities!

Me: (Laughing.) Yes, I know. But when you grow up, you will have an overbite that no one can notice. I didn't like my smile even though my teeth were straight. I got braces when I was thirty-two years old. After I wore out my retainer, a tooth here and there has shifted, not as straight as they once were.

Little Girl: Now, how in the world do bracelets fix your teeth? And, what's a retainer?

Me: Not bracelets. Braces the Orthodontist puts on your teeth to make them straight. Then after the teeth are straight, he takes the braces off. The retainer is a clear plastic piece that goes on your teeth to help keep your teeth straight.

Little Girl: Ortho… What now? Nevermind. I'm not even going to ask.

Me: Ok. Orthodontist. A dentist who specializes in fixing teeth. Is that better?

Little Girl: Yea, that's better.

Me: So, now you understand why you should stop sucking your thumb, right?

Little Girl: I guess… You wanna know why I'm called Hincha?

Me: Go ahead. Something tells me you're going to tell me anyway.

Little Girl: Yup, I am. Because, my skin color isn't white or brown. I guess that's another thing wrong with me. Besides, sometimes, I'm naughty.

Me: Well, you have a beautiful skin color. Why are you naughty?

Little Girl: Because, when my big sister tells lies about me, they always believe her. And, I get in trouble even when I don't do anything wrong. I am either playing with my toy piano or with my younger brother. She never gets in trouble. I think it's because she's brown and writes and eats with her right hand. She doesn't get called many names like me. Nothing is wrong with her. So, I may as well get myself in trouble.

Me: Hey, there's nothing wrong with you. You are perfect the way you are. You need to believe and know that you are pretty and loved. You want to live a full, abundant, happy life.

Little Girl: Pretty? Then, why do the girls at church say I'm ugly and look like Medusa? Whatever that means. I just know it's not good. They point at my hair and laugh. My hair gets frizzy, and kids at school also make fun of me, especially when my two front teeth fell out. I was the only one whose teeth were missing on picture day. Mami straightened my hair with an iron for my picture. The picture lady gave us a small black comb. Then when it was my turn, she told me to say cheese, smile, and show my teeth. I looked at her like she was crazy. I smiled with my mouth closed. Boy, brushing my teeth was hard. The toothbrush kept falling through where my teeth used to be. I was so happy when my new teeth grew in, because brushing my teeth wasn't so hard to do.

Me: Again, there's nothing wrong with you. Kids can be mean. My older daughter had a picture day when she also lost her two front teeth. She actually listened to the picture lady. It was right around Christmas time. I wrote on the back of her pictures, "All I want for Christmas is my front teeth." (There was silence.) What's wrong?

Little Girl: Nothing.

Me: Tell me. A minute ago, you were excited, and now you got quiet on me.

Little Girl: Fine, I don't like Christmas.

Me: Why?

Little Girl: I don't understand why we have to go to Mami's brother's house every Christmas Eve after church. They have this big Christmas tree that touches the ceiling. There are lots of presents around the tree in the living room. We have to open presents at midnight. My cousin and her sister get a lot of presents. While my brothers, sister and I have to sit there and watch them open up all their presents. We only get one present. Then on Christmas morning, my parents go into the closet and bring out a toy for each of us. They say it's from Santa Claus. But if it's from Santa, why aren't they wrapped in Christmas paper? And, why do we only get one toy? Other kids get a lot of toys. I don't even like birthdays. It's just another day. We only get a cake, not even presents. Last birthday, my Mami's brother came over. I was playing outside. He had this huge birthday card. I was so happy. I have never seen anything like it. I ran to him, thinking it was for me. He laughed and said it wasn't for me.

Me: I'm so sorry. I have something to tell you that will make you happy. I never introduced myself. (I whispered my name in her ear)

Little Girl: No way. That's my name! You can't have my name. I'm the only one with that name.

Me: (I stood in front of her, looking at her light golden brown eyes piercing at me.) You won't believe me. But, you see this? (I pointed to my forehead slightly above my left eyebrow near the center.)

Little Girl: I have that, too. (She points to hers on her forehead.)

Me: I know! I can tell you how you got that chickenpox mark! (Her eyes got bigger, and her pupils dilated.) Papi sat you on his lap when you got the chickenpox, and he peeled it off your forehead.

Little Girl: Wait a minute. You know my Papi, too?

Me: Yes. He's my Papi, too.

Little Girl: I don't want to be rude. You're pretty and all. But, you look way older than my Papi. There's no way he can't be your Papi.

Me: (Laughing) Ok now. I'm not that old. Seriously, listen to me.

Little Girl: I'm listening, so you can push me again.

Me: I am your future self.

Little Girl: Future what? You mean to tell me I will be pretty when I grow old like you?

Me: Hey, hey. I'm not old, missy. You're already pretty and funny.

Little Girl: Thanks. You wanna know something else?

Me: Go ahead and tell me.

Little Girl: I can beat up boys. (She says it like it's a good thing.)

Me: Well, that's not a good thing to do.

Little Girl: Only the ones that mess with my little brother. I'm the only one who messes with him. But, you knew that already. Right? Because, you're me. But an old me. (Laughing.) Can you push me higher this time?

Me: I will push you, but not too high. Funny girl.

Little Girl: Why not?

Me: Because, I don't want you to get hurt or break any bones.

Little Girl: Ha! Break some bones. I never break any bones. I climb trees and jump high.

Me: (I mumbled.) Lord, knows how many dangerous things I did. Thank God I didn't break any bones.

Little Girl: What did you say?

Me: Nothing. I was talking to myself.

Little Girl: Hey, I thought I was you. I couldn't hear you.

Me: Yea, but talking to myself is like saying my thoughts out loud to me.

Little Girl: Aye, Aye. You're confusing me. You just told me that I'm you, and you are me. Now, you're talking to yourself, but not me, me. Grown-ups are confusing.

Me: (Laughing) Yes, we are. You are right. You are me, and I am you. I was just saying that you're a tough cookie.

Little Girl: A… what? Did you just call me a cookie?

Me: (Laughing) It's just a figure of speech.

Little Girl: A figure of what, now?

Me: "It's… (She cuts me off.)

Little Girl: I get it, grown-up talk.

Me: Yes. Now, it's my turn to tell you what I can do or rather am doing. I am an actress in movies, commercials, music videos, and more cool stuff.

Little Girl: What? No way, José!

Me: Yepper.

Little Girl: You mean, every time I wished I would be on television, it comes true?

Me: Yup! And, you heard me tell you about my two daughters. I have four children and seven grandchildren.

Little Girl: Woah! That's a full house.

Me: (I then pulled out my cell phone from my fanny pack to show her my pictures in my gallery.) Here, let me show you something.

Little Girl: Uhmmm. Aren't you too old to be playing with toys?

Me: This isn't a toy. It's a phone.

Little Girl: Phones are plugged into walls.

Me: This is a future phone without cords. It's called a cell phone. Look at this. (I showed her my pictures in my gallery.)

Little Girl: They are cute. Hey, she kinda looks like me.

Me: Yes, she does. That's my seven-year-old granddaughter.

Little Girl: Hey, wait a minute. I didn't see your husband.

Me: Well, I don't have one just yet. When the time is right, I will. Hey, look at the rain clouds. Let's get you home before it starts to rain.

Little Girl: Ok.

Me: Oh, yeah. On our twenty-fifth birthday, we had our first birthday party. It was fun. It was a last minute, a little crazy, but a memorable one.

Little Girl: What does it mean to be a little crazy?

Me: Oh, uhm… Just a lot of silly friends, that's what I meant.

Little Girl: Really? Did we get a lot of presents, balloons, cake, and ice cream?

Me: No presents or ice cream. But food, cake, music, and..."

Little Girl: And what?

Me: Uhmmm. Water, lots of water.

Little Girl: Ooh. So, do we have more parties?

Me: No, we don't. I'm happy with a cake and being around those who love me. It's not about presents. It's about Love!

Little Girl: Awe. No more parties?

Me: Hey, did you feel that? I felt a raindrop. (I looked up to see the sky. It was full of dark clouds and looked like it was night.) I'm glad I brought my umbrella.

Little Girl: Nope, I didn't feel anything.

Me: I need you to do me a favor. When you're scared, pray to God.

Little Girl: Oh, I always pray. Mami makes sure I pray every morning before I leave for school and before going to bed. But, you already knew that, right?

Me: Yes. God lives inside you. (I pointed to her heart.)

Little Girl: I'm too little. God is a giant. He can't live inside me. I'm not a house that sounds crazy.

Me: Ok, but He really does. You can't see Him. You can only feel Him. Just like the ocean is a large body of water on Earth, it's everywhere, even inside our bodies.

Little Girl: Duh. Everyone knows that when you drink water, it goes inside your body.

Me: Yes, that's true. However, our bodies have water already, and we have to keep drinking water to keep it healthy. As I was saying. Water is everywhere, and it's needed everywhere. Plants and animals need water to live. There's water in the clouds, mist, fog, rivers, and so on. It's the one element of the Earth that can take any form. Well, that's how God is. He is a large source of power and inside everyone, every living being.

Little Girl: God can't be inside of me. I'm only six years old.

Me: Well, he does, and you will understand it one day. God loves everything created in his image with agape Love.

Little Girl: AGAPE, what now? I can't learn your big words. If I talk like you in school, the kids will look at me crazy. You can keep talking like that, but not me. It's too hard for me. Remember, I'm only six years old.

Me: (Laughing) Ok, ok. It means unconditional love. God loves all, no matter what. Call on Him and the angels whenever you're scared. Or even just to say, "Thank you" for everything good that happens to you. Oh, and don't talk to strangers!

Little Girl: But, you were a stranger at first, and now you are me, and I am you. Hmmmm, but what if the stranger is the future husband?

Me: Listen to me. No!

Little Girl: Ok, ok. I was just kidding. I got it, no strangers.

Me: Also, don't tell anyone about this.

Little girl: I won't. No one listens to me anyways.

Me: One more thing. Close your eyes. (Suddenly, the rain stops.) No peeking, eyes completely closed.

(She closes her eyes, smiling with her cute dimples. A bright golden beaming light came down from the sky, shining on her from head to toe. Then,

Spirit, angels, and my ancestors all create a clear invisible protection bubble around her. Only those who are assigned to help her grow through experiences and lessons are allowed inside her world. She is divinely protected.)

Me: Ok, now you can open your eyes, pretty girl.

Little Girl: What happened?

Me: How do you feel?

Little Girl: Good! Look at the rainbow!

Me: Oh, wow! It's a double rainbow. That's beautiful!

(We both look up, admiring the beautiful double rainbow in the sky.)

Me: Come, give me a hug.

(We embraced each other with a tight hug.)

Me: I love you! (I kissed her forehead. I saw a spark in her eyes.)

Little Girl: (She placed her left hand on my right cheek.) Be good to yourself. I love you, too.

(Then, she jumps up and waves with a huge smile. However, she wasn't waving at me.)

Me: Wait a minute. (I looked next to me and saw Spirit, the angels, and our ancestors are all smiling.)

They: She called us before you called us!

Little Girl: Took you long enough. (She giggles.)

Me: Wow! Did I just get played by a six-year-old? (They all began to laugh.)

They: We needed you to heal your inner child so that we can move on to the next level. You have work to do. We can see you're becoming extraordinary!

(She began to ascend. I felt my heart opening up, much like a hibiscus flower blossoming. Suddenly, it felt like my heart was sucking her in like a vacuum cleaner. My younger self was inside my heart. I felt this warm sensation of peace within. Then, I felt strong vibrations underneath my feet. The ground was slightly trembling. I turned around, and the entire street was full of my ancestors and more angles floating in the open space.)

They: Know that you're highly ranked in the spiritual realm. Though you feel like you're alone, you are never alone. We are here with you all the way. (I felt a wet drop on my cheek and thought it was the rain. Suddenly, heavy tears came down. I cried, I cried, because I always felt like I was alone, and they knew.)

When I opened my eyes, I found myself lying on my bed. Then I heard a loud buzzing sound. It was my alarm clock going off. When I was fully awakened, I felt my satin pillowcase was wet. I stood on my feet, yawned, and stretched. I walked to the bathroom, turned on the light, and looked at myself in the mirror. I could not help to notice one teardrop hanging from my left eyelash. Apparently, I had cried so hard in my sleep that my pillow was wet from my tears. I said thank you to God for his love. I said, "I love you," to my reflection in the mirror. I told myself I would try to do better than yesterday.

My Ancestors

I understood my parents did their best with what they knew based on their experiences. As an adult, my father shared his good and bad childhood memories. He grew up with both parents, five sisters, and three brothers. He was raised on a large farm in the mountains of Puerto Rico, near the rainforest. My father grew up learning how to grow crops and raise chickens, roosters, cows, pigs, and buffalos. His oldest brother passed away as a toddler. Their religion was Pentecostal. I was so disappointed, because he raised me in a Pentecostal religion, and he did not understand how to heal and let go of resentment and past pain. Why be a fanatic in the church, but not understand the purpose of being and trusting God to heal the pain?

I grew up not knowing my father's family that lived on the east coast of the States. I have yet to meet most of my aunts, uncles, and cousins. Through social media, I have been able to connect with a few now with the new world. When I was a child, I visited Puerto Rico and met some relatives there. As adults, my father and his siblings did not speak to each other; in real-time, they are still in a feud. I remember seeing my uncles come for my baby brother's funeral, and they left immediately and went back to New Jersey. They seem to live in resentment from their past.

Resentment has created chronic illness and possibly a generational curse. Unfortunately, my father was recently diagnosed with Vascular Dementia and has a few chronic illnesses. He is in a childlike state of mind. It breaks my heart to see him this way. He has moments when he does not recognize me in person or in a photo. It is heartbreaking when seeing my father decline. He knows he has a daughter with my name and recognizes me over the phone. But he still remains in a negative mindset.

I enjoy hearing about my parents' past, because it gave me a better understanding of who they are and who I am becoming. My paternal grandfather's mother was a singer and musician. He was a singer and guitarist himself. He taught all of his sons how to play the guitar. My father also taught my siblings and I the basic tunes on the guitar. My younger brother is the only one who went further with this skill. He mastered the guitar and taught himself how to play the lead guitar as well as the piano. On the other hand, I had no interest when my dad was teaching me as a young girl. I now wish I had taken more interest then.

My father dropped out of school in the fourth grade. He began working around ten years of age. He would also help my grandmother get water for the family and help my grandfather with the farm. When he earned a living, he would contribute his earnings with his parents. He would help purchase rice, lard, and essentials for the household. My father shared very few good memories from his childhood. He said I reminded him of his maternal grandmother. She was a beautiful Italian woman with black hair.

My grandfather's father passed away when he was younger, so he was raised by a single mother. He would go with her to deliver babies. I enjoyed hearing the stories of her riding on a horse with a lantern to the homes of expecting mothers to deliver unborn children, a midwife. She also delivered all her grandchildren.

My father resents his father. My grandfather passed away in July 2021 at the age of one hundred and six. May he rest in peace. He lived a long life and experienced two pandemics during his lifetime. My father is still hurt from his past trauma and reminisces about those childhood memories. That affected him mentally, emotionally, and physically.

When I visit my father, he remains stuck in the past. He is aware that his mental state is not well. I asked him a few questions about my grandparents, and he consciously answered them. Then he said I was asking more questions than a lawyer with a laugh. He still has his sense of humor. He said to me that he no longer lives in that world he once knew. I asked him what world he lives in now. He said he would rather not talk about it, but it's too complicated and not a good one. He said he was cursed. Though, he is in this state of mind. He shares a lot of wisdom. I have expressed to him to let go of his past. He is set in his ways and has no idea how to make that happen. He has not done the work to heal his pain, that his soul is carrying. I wish he will heal all his heartaches and understand this is a direct connection to God for his freedom. My father is a prisoner in his own body. It is terrifying to see him in this way. I pray for his mental, emotional, physical, and spiritual healing.

Once again, he was talking about all his resentment toward his father. This was the first time I expressed to him the names he participated in calling me, that affected me as a young girl. I had forgiven them. I did not realize; at the time, it developed into insecurities. He did not recall it and was surprised that he was a part of it. I wanted him to forgive his father and let go of his past. He was so childlike at that moment. He was apologetic and humble. I then realized it was not the true being inside him. It was his hurt ego that took over him. I told him that I found my peace, forgave, and still loved them. I felt like I was speaking to a toddler. I wanted to help him, but it was too late. I found my peace years ago. I did not want to be like my father in this way.

I grew up hearing him manifesting sickness. In his younger years, he was healthy and strong. My mother always said he had a powerful tongue. Every time he spoke of something, it would become a reality. He spoke about every illness he has. I did not understand the power he had within him, and I do not think he even knew himself..

I appreciate all that he did for his family. I loved that he was a provider. However, he was not entirely in the present moment. He did not know how to become vulnerable, letting go of his past. Be receptive to forgiveness and heal his pain. I always saw my father being grumpy or easily irritated. My father never healed from his past pain. He is almost eighty years old and still burdened. I wish I knew what I know now and wish I could have influenced my father to heal his heart and mind. But he has been complacent and set in his way. I still pray for his healing and peace of mind.

My Mother's History

My mother grew up in a town in Puerto Rico with her parents and her six siblings. My grandmother gave birth to four sons and three daughters. My grandmother's three pregnancies with the girls were each twins with a boy. Unfortunately, the male babies did not survive during labor. My mother was one of the twins that survived. My grandfather found unclaimed land and built a shack in the mountains on an open steep area surrounded by fertile land. He raised cows, pigs, rabbits, goats, and chickens and sold them for survival. They were the only ones living in that area. It was paradise in my mother's eyes. They lived an abundant life with natural resources.

However, they did not have access to water or electricity. They were a long distance from the water supply. My grandfather planted every seed;

guava, oranges, guanabana, mango, yuca, yams, pumpkin, green plantains, green bananas, and tobacco. My mother shares that she had a great childhood. On a rainy day, she and her siblings would play in the rain enjoying nature. She is the baby in the family. My mother and her siblings are very close. They all still live in Puerto Rico. She was raised Catholic, then converted to Pentecostal in her teenage years.

My grandparents were divorced when my mother was seven years old. My mother did not see her father as much growing up. Though my grandparents were first cousins, they parted ways. My mother's grandmothers were sisters from Spain. My mother's, mother, father was Indian, and my mother's father, father was Italian. I never met my grandfather. In recent years, my mom has shared her happiest memories. Daily, my grandmother and uncles would walk far to get water for them to drink, bathe and cook with. My mother's oldest brother went to live with my grandfather. The second oldest brother stayed to help. He worked as a carpenter at age eighteen. He learned how to build homes and taught his younger brothers when they were of age.

My grandmother was getting older and could not keep up with the daily routine of bringing water back up to the shack for everyone to use. My mother's brother found a closer location near the city with easy access to water and electricity. He used the materials from the shack and reminisce materials from his job and built a small house with three bedrooms for them to live away from the mountains. They no longer had the fruits of the land. Their survival was challenging. They now had to buy food.

Once my father became an adult, he moved to the States to find a better job to work and send money back home. He lived with a friend, and based on the story, his friend was unfaithful to his wife. The living arrangement was disrupted. My father was living on the streets. When I heard this story from my aunt, my eyes teared up. She described my father alone on the streets of NYC, not being able to speak English. A friend from his hometown ran into him. My dad got sick and was taken back to Puerto Rico and hospitalized. My grandfather had my dad admitted to a private hospital. She said my dad lost a lot of weight. Since then, he has developed nervousness. My aunt describes my father as a good son and brother. My mom also confirmed this story to be true. She shared that my dad told her about this unfortunate experience. My grandmother slaughtered and cooked fresh chicken to cook, homemade chicken soup for my father. I grew up believing this soup was healing. She wanted to nurse him back to his natural state of health. He then returned back to the States. He then met my mother at a church in Philadelphia. It all began to make sense to me why my dad was the way he was.

My Father - The Provider

My father worked hard to provide, and I appreciate my parents. I had the privilege of being raised in a three-bedroom house with a fully fenced backyard, basement, and bathroom indoors. We had the necessities. My parents played kickball and hide and seek with my siblings and me. My father would take us to the park when the weather permitted. He grew corn and pumpkins in our backyard. But during Halloween time, the pumpkins were stolen.

As mentioned, my father sold the house due to the break-ins. We lived in an apartment for one year. Then, my father purchased a two-story house. We had a big apple tree in the backyard. I grew up with two older siblings and a younger brother. My baby brother passed away when he was three years old; rest in peace. My upbringing was a mixture of Pentecostal religion and Puerto Rican culture. This lifestyle was a level-up for my parents. My parents were strict with the religion, and I could not wear pants. Winters were brutal walking in the cold, but they let me run free outdoors.

My favorite memory my mother has shared with me is when my oldest brother was born on their first anniversary. During labor, the Doctor said to push. My parents did not speak English. However, he understood the word push. He put his hands behind my mother to help her push. They both laughed when they shared this moment.

The day my mother and brother were discharged, my father butchered one of the chickens he had raised and made homemade chicken soup for my mother. When she came home with their new baby, they had no clue how to be parents. Being a parent and raising children does not come with a manual. They learned along the way, as most parents do, including me. It amazes me how animals seem to understand their purpose in the world more than human beings, except when we grow from newborn to toddler. At this age, we have a free mind and are in touch with our natural instinct.

My mother was a stay at home mom. However, after a few years we moved into a bigger house with a fenced yard in a nicer neighborhood. My father was laid off, so my mother had to start working to help pay the bills. My father soon started working at an industrial laundry, and my mother soon joined him. I watched them struggle to provide. I wanted to work for something other than a company that would lay me off. I did not want to worry about finances as I watched my parents do. I learned to save money as a young girl and watched and observed grown-ups. I wanted to live a different way of life. I always tend to do the opposite of others.

My Youthful History

I was the one out of my siblings who did most of the cleaning. On Saturdays, everyone cleaned. I learned how to cook when I was eleven. I burned my first pot of white rice. My father put onions in the rice to eliminate the burnt taste. I was the only one who would help my mother wash clothes on a washboard in a silver bucket filled with water in the basement. Ringing the clothes was not a fun thing to do. Then, we would hang the clothes outside on the pole lines with wooden clothespins.

If I was not in the kitchen helping my mother, I was in the streets playing with my brother and the kids in the neighborhood. We would climb and jump the sheds and monkey bars. One of my friends in my neighborhood had a bike. I learned to ride a bike with her on the seat I was standing, pedaling. Sometimes, there would be three or four of us on the bike. I was the one who stood up pedaling, the other one sitting on the handlebar, then one was on the seat, and one standing on the back tire holding on to the one sitting on the seat. I don't know how we managed to fit like monkeys on the bike. But we did. We always had to be home before it was dark. We enjoyed Summer time.

It was towards the end of my sixth-grade year. I used to walk everywhere alone, or sometimes with siblings, but mostly alone. However, one particular day, I walked with my friend. She was one year older than I was. It was the end of the day. We missed the school bus, because we were at the library next to the school and had lost track of time. I lived on the east side of town. Our school was on the south side of town. My friend's aunt lived fifteen minutes from my house. We headed towards her aunt's house. She knew her way around the town for a twelve years old girl. That was an experience for me, because it was a chance for me to learn my way around that side of town.

It was a warm day, so we took our shoes off and walked barefoot. It took us hours to get to my house. The school bus ride was only thirty minutes to my house. I got home before my parents, so I did not get in trouble. That was my first time walking a long distance as a child without an adult.

I remember being in the crib and sharing a room with my older sister, how my parents' room was next door with a closet between the rooms, and that we lived downstairs.

As an adult, I have shared my childhood memories with my mother. I told her about the day, she was lying on the sofa, and I was standing next to her. I remember I was able to rest my arm on the seat part of the sofa. At that moment, my father came home from work. She says I was three years old. She was surprised at how detailed my memory was for such a young age.

Though I grew up with both my parents having a lack of mindset. Deep down I knew there was something of the opposite out there. I truly appreciate my parents as they sacrificed, provided and protected us. Such as the male owl is a provider. He attracts the female owl to a nest and offers her food. When she accepts his offer, they mate. Then they each provide and protect their offspring, until they are independent to find their own hunting territory.

Poor Community

I grew up with low self-esteem. I did not like myself, because I was criticized about everything that had to do with my body, from head to toe, ever since I was a child. I would hear adults say comments at home, school, and church. They would point out that I was pigeon-toed, and my varicose veins would look bad as I aged. I became easily irritated and resentful. I was especially ridiculed because I was slim with a big booty and my skin tone with unruly, frizzy, curly hair. Starting at the age of ten, my mother had me wear a girdle. I was not overweight, I was slim with a big buttock. I was teased about my muscular legs and big buttock by almost everyone my entire life, until it became popular.

I could not escape it. I was ridiculed by so many. I was ashamed of my body. I remember always hiding from people and covering my face with my hands. I was extremely timid, afraid and uneasy. So, of course, any child would believe something was wrong with them. It all began to make sense why I did not have confidence.

By this time, I was conformed to self-sabotaging with fear. My insecure personality developed based on my community's influences and expectations. I had so many conditioned beliefs about my outer image that I became a pleaser, afraid to disappoint others. I wanted acceptance. For so long, I attracted low vibrations connections, because I was omitting that same low frequency.

Living in Truth

As an adult, I still did not fit in and continued to be a loner playing it small. However, I was not created to play it small. I embraced all my experiences during my primitive years. It took some time as an adult to heal, but I finally realized nothing was wrong with me, only my way of thinking and feeling. Everything in my foundational experience was not by mistake. It was for a reason. I challenged myself to focus on my light within. I avoided focusing on what I did not have. I deleted the old stories in my mind about not feeling worthy enough to fit in with my own kind, or anyone for that matter. I realized I was a perfect being, imperfect. That is how I was created. This was my vessel, and I had to treat myself better.

I learned to become resilient and stopped my self-sabotaging behaviors. I no longer wanted to live in a place of resentment. I wanted better for myself. I owed it to myself. I began to work hard on my healing and accepting my outer body as a gift from The Divine. My inner world began to reflect my external world. I accepted all my innate flaws and began to understand that I am a spiritual being inside a human body, experiencing life on Earth with an expression of God. I am not a body. My body is me. I am one with God. I decided to change my story in order to change my reality.

Psalm 34:18
"The LORD is close to the brokenhearted and saves those who are crushed in spirit."

Day 

Emotional Bondage Kept Me Hostage

I found myself in a daze and heard a familiar voice say, "Wakey, wakey. Yoo-hoo. Snap out of it." I looked to my right and saw God sitting in the passenger seat of this high-tech prestige vehicle with a touch screen and hologram. The seats were white and made of lambskin with a comfortable soft touch. I had fallen asleep sitting in the driver's seat. The sunroof was open, and the interior was made of vibranium, crystalline, and gold. It sort of reminded me of one of Princess Shuri, King T'Challa's teenage sister's, technology designs in the movie "Wakanda" It was something I had never seen in this lifetime.

As I take in this luxurious high-tech prestige vehicle, I hear God say, Mi Hija. You are in such a dream state. Look, you didn't even notice her right over there." He points to this teenage girl, dragging her feet with her shoulders down as she crosses the street. I looked at her and then did a double take and looked at God.

"Wait, what are you wearing? And why are you dressed like that?" He had the seat reclined back, wearing a white baseball cap, plain white t-shirt, dark blue ripped jeans, and white Nike sneakers. "What? You don't think I look good in this outfit?" He responded as He checked Himself in the mirror. "I think I look good, and besides, I am dressed because I created you in my image so that you can be an expression of me and experience everything I have created. Therefore, with you being here on earth, I can experience it all. Geesh… You have been such a hermit for so long. You have not been dressing in style with all those clothes in your closet. You do not go anywhere. It's been pretty boring lately. I had high expectations for you. However, I don't know about that anymore, Missy. Ehhhh, Stop worrying about what I am wearing and go talk to her. She needs your help in becoming extraordinary!"

As I was trying to figure out how to open the door, I replied, "Okay, I will." God said, "Use your fingerprint. It was designed for you alone and, of course, yours truly." Then he winks at me. I place my index finger on the door, and it opens slowly. As I'm getting out, I hear the vehicle greet me by name and say goodbye with some bachata music in the background. Oh my! A talking vehicle with music. I'm starting to feel like I was in a remake of Knight Rider. I ran up to the teenage girl.

She looks at me and says, "Hey, you're back." Her expression was extremely gloomy, with low vibrations. She didn't seem like that witty, funny little girl I met from ten years ago.

Me: Hey. What's wrong?

Teenage Girl: I hate my life. But, you should know this. So, why even bother asking?

Me: (I sighed.) Oh, I thought the last time I saw you, I told you to call on God.

Teenage Girl: I did. He ignored me!

Me: What do you mean He ignored you? He never ignored you.

Teenage Girl: Well, He did. I begged Him to heal Benji. I even spoke in tongues. And, God still let him die." (She burst into tears, and my heart felt the pain. I hugged her tight.)

Me: Sweetheart, God did not ignore you. He did not let him die. He is now one of your angels. He is watching over you. He still lives. Just not here in the flesh.

Teenage Girl: I had a nightmare. The lady from church, who died, came into my dream and told me she was taking him with her. And, I saw him in the casket. I did not tell anyone. Maybe, if I did, he would still be alive. He died the same month I was born and the 25th day he was born. It's just not fair. Just the other day, I was walking to the corner store, and this little boy around his age shouted at me, "Hey, you with the big titties!" How is it that my brother could not even talk because of his brain tumor? He dies, and these bad kids get to live.

Me: I know it is not fair. I miss him, too. But, I found peace, and now I know he is watching over us right now. Listen to me. I need you to go see a doctor. Mami keeps your health insurance in her wallet. You are having a baby, and she will give you a reason to want to live.

Teenage Girl: What? No! I can not be pregnant. I'm too young. They will kill me. (She begins to cry.)

Me: I promise you, they will be disappointed. However, they will be ok. Trust me. Okay?

Teenage Girl: OK! I guess. (I hugged her.)

Me: Don't ever give up. Please keep getting up every time you fall. Promise me that?

Teenage Girl: Ok, I will. Thank you. (She placed her hand on her stomach and proceeded to walk home. I then walked back to my luxurious vehicle. I was ready to take it for a spin. As I get closer, the passenger side door opens up. There was God, sitting in the driver's seat. He has a sense of humor.)

Me: I thought you said this was customized just for me.

God: Yeah. You're not fully present or awakened. I need to take over. You have been operating looking in the rearview mirror and dazing too much. I need you to be in the present moment at all times. Look straight ahead and around you. Only look in the rearview mirror for a quick moment when you need to see something from your past that you have learned to move up to the next lane.

Me: (I sighed.) I understand.

(I sat in the passenger seat, and God took off at full speed. My head hit the back of the headrest. I said, "Hey, I thought You knew how to handle this vehicle smoothly." God replied, "I do. But now, I am late for my next appointment." (He winks at me with a sparkle in his eyes. I just smiled back at Him.)

Held Hostage

I then took a deep breath and exhaled. I opened my eyes, and there I was, sitting on my balcony. The sun was so bright, shining on my face. I was surrounded by my beautiful yellow, red, and orange hibiscus trees, white gardenia trees, and palm trees. I saw a hummingbird fly toward my yellow hibiscus tree. My heart became so heavy as I remembered why I was so hurt and furious with God.

I remembered so much fear, resentment, and pain in my life from my youth. My cousin was murdered in Puerto Rico when I was nine years old. I believe he was thirteen when this happened. All I could remember was my father receiving a call. While he was on the phone, he dropped to the floor crying. That was heartbreaking to see. No one likes to see their parents cry. He and his friends had gotten into trouble in school, and he confessed what they did when his teacher interrogated him. Later, his friends lured and murdered him. He was not a swimmer, and they pushed him into the river and left him to drown. Children killing children. That day, I learned not to trust anyone near water and not to snitch on anyone. Then our family dogs died when I was eleven years old. It was a gloomy period in my life.

When I was thirteen years old, one of my best friends was raped and murdered on her way to school. She was feisty, tough, and outspoken. I still did not fit in with my peers, but she was super cool with me. We would meet in the mornings at the corner of my street. We would walk to and from school together. Throughout my youth years, I also had classmates who committed suicide and some that were murdered. I was extremely quiet and avoided drama. That is how I became reserved as I got older. I recently became aware that I was always being divinely protected. I have experienced mourning loss at an early age. As an adult, my cousin on my father's side committed suicide. Recently my aunt called to inform me that my cousin was murdered a few days ago. I could not share this with my father's present state. Sometimes I feel like my life is a film on the big screen with unknown writers.

As I got older, I would beg my mother to have another baby. When she got pregnant with my baby brother, I was so happy. Finally, my wish came true. I always loved kids. I would volunteer at the church nursery to play with the kids. When my mother was expecting, I walked with her to her doctor's appointments. My father was working, so he could not take days off.

We were walking to the store one day, and a twenty-dollar bill was on the sidewalk. My mother dropped down so fast and picked it up. I was shocked. She struggled to tie her shoes all this time, and I helped her. She did not seem to struggle to bend down for that twenty-dollar bill, though.

My baby brother was born. He was such a joy. As time passed, my mom expressed to the doctor that she noticed his delayed development, compared to us at his age. The doctor said some babies develop slower than others. She also expressed that he had a big lump on his neck. Again, this doctor said it was normal, just a swollen gland. My baby brother was diagnosed with a brain tumor on his 1st birthday. He had an emergency brain surgery. I remember arriving in his room, and he came to me. I held him until it was time for his surgery. He was hospitalized for a long time. My mother never left the hospital.

Around this time, I became rebellious, began to skip school, and learned a lot of mischievous things. After a while, I was tired of getting in trouble at home because of my sister. She was always lying about me, to my parents. They would always believe her.

One day, my dad came home from work. I was yelled at for no reason, and my dad hit me. My sister had her music playing loud and blamed it on me. Of course, he believed her over me. At that moment, I made up my mind to run away. I packed a plastic bag and walked to my friend's house. It took me one hour to walk. I was so used to walking everywhere alone at an early age.

My friend hid me in the attic. My parents knew where my friend lived, and they sent the police to my friend's house. I could hear them through the vent. But, I was just sick and tired of getting in trouble for no reason, so

I remained quiet. My friend would come to the attic and bring me food. I slept on the floor with a pillow and blanket. A couple of days went by, and I decided to return home. When I got home, my parents were nicer to me. I returned to school, and my classmates told me my parents had come looking for me.

During my teenage years, I liked to wear eyeliner and bracelets. I still could not wear pants. However, that went against the Pentecostal religion. Eventually, my parents accepted me and allowed me to wear eyeliner and bracelets.

I witnessed many things that weren't Godly at the church, so I didn't like going. However, I would in order to help my mother at the church when she needed me to. I would help my mom with my baby brother and carry his oxygen tank.

I remember one particular time during a weeknight service. The co-pastor was preaching and shouted, "There's a demon in here." I was afraid to look around. Holy crap! He pointed towards me and said it was me. He called out my parents' names, telling the congregation their daughter was the demon. He didn't even know my first name.

That's right. He called me a demon just because I was wearing eyeliner. I was so offended; the nerve of this man to judge me as a teenager. Ironically when his children got older, they were involved with drug dealers and left the church. That is why it is not good to judge others by their appearances. This church always had bats flying in the sanctuary. It was scary, especially when the preacher was always preaching fear.

During this period, my life was hectic. I did not know how to control my emotions. Plus, I was experiencing puberty. My baby brother's health got worse, and my mother slept at the hospital with him. She never left his side. Sometimes, my siblings and I chose to sleep in the lounge area of the hospital. We would shower there as well. We practically lived there.

When my brother was discharged and returned home, he cried every night from the pain. He would constantly rub his head. There was nothing we could do to alleviate his pain. One of the side effects of his illness was that he could not speak. This prevented him from expressing himself verbally. During the night, I would wake up and help comfort my baby brother.

My uncle on Mom's side would make fun of my baby brother for losing his hair. I guess he was trying to make light of the situation. He was always making fun of my dad and telling inappropriate jokes. I was not fond of him. I did not think it was funny. My baby brother lost his hair due to chemotherapy and radiation.

I would sometimes go hang out with my best friend to get away from it all. I would either ride a bike, sit under a tree or walk around the neighborhood. Almost every time on my way back home, I would hear the ambulance sirens. I knew it was for my baby brother. I would run if I was walking or ride the bike fast to get home. When I finally reached my home, there it was. The ambulance parked right in front of my house, and my parents were panicking and crying.

I learned CPR during this time. I remembered he had a shunt and ivy in his chest. I was careful with him. When I was home, I was the one who was calm to perform this when his lips turned blue while having seizures. He was constantly going back to the hospital on a regular basis. After a while, this was our new normal.

To deal with all of life's traumas, I skipped classes and began hanging out with bad influences. I got into so much trouble in school. It was normal for the sentries to chase me down the school hallways. I ran out of the building so fast they could not catch me. There were times that I would tell my teachers I did not feel good, so that I would have an excuse not to be in class and go to the nurse. Ironically, the nurse would take my temperature, and I did have a fever. I was able to lie on the cot to avoid exams. I did not like going to school.

I went from being a studious student to a bad student. Sometimes, I would sit in class miserable and just wish for a blackout so we could all go home. Ironically, all the lights would go out, and we would get to go home. Or, I would wish someone would call in a bomb threat or a fire drill. It would also happen as if I had a genie lamp. It became normal for me to say this and wish for it, and it came true.

Everyone knew that my brother was sick, even up to my high school years. So much so, that it's crazy how when I got my high school transcript, they had his diagnosis and death in the notes. One morning, I did not feel like going to school. I was the only one at home. My homeroom teacher came all the way to my house. She knocked on my door. I did not open it. I heard her calling my name. She said she knew I was home. It was crazy to me that this woman took it upon herself to come to my house and get me for school. She was determined in encouraging me to attend school. That same day my classmate came to my house with two other girls. She suggested we go hang out downtown. We gathered all the soda cans for a 5-cent refund. We went to Super Duper Grocery and cashed them in. We caught the city bus downtown.

That was my first time on a city bus. I was unaware of where we were going. We ended up in the office of a middle school. We were signing as tardy and when the receptionist asked my name. I responded with the name Cecily Jones. She said I must have been a good kid because she did not recognize me. Somehow the sentries of the school knew we were not students from the school. We ran out of the building running down the street so fast.

I was 13 years old, and I had no idea where I was. I made sure as I ran, I kept behind my friend. She obviously knew her way around the west side of town. We made it back to my house and went to school during the 6th period. That day I learned a lot of mischievous things.

Backtracking to when I was in the seventh grade. I shared lockers with my so-called close friend. Her friend stole my winter boots. Then she played dumb when I asked her where my boots were. I had to walk home in the cold winter in regular shoes. My father tried his best to buy us one new outfit and a pair of boots every school year. I had to deal with not having boots during that winter season. A few months later, her friend was walking to school with my winter boots while I walked to school during the cold winter with holes in the bottom of my soles. I learned not to leave what I considered valuable in a shared locker. I forgave the girl who stole my boots, and later we became amicable when I became rebellious. She was the one I learned to skip school.

Towards the end of my eighth-grade year, I was so rebellious. I always got suspended or in school detention for skipping classes. During school detention, I would ask to use the restroom when I knew my friends would be on their way to class, so I would hang out with them between classes. Then, I would go back to the detention classroom. I was hiding my feelings about my friends' betrayal, so I acted as if I did not care. I buried the feelings and moved on. I had the I do not care attitude. However, because of that attitude, I was not making smart choices.

I almost failed the ninth grade. I had never failed a grade. So in my tenth-grade year, I decided to straighten up. I was embarrassed to be in a ninth-grade homeroom with tenth-grade classes and an eleventh-grade Spanish class. I asked what options were available to get into the tenth-grade homeroom with my friends. My Global Studies teacher advised me to retake the final exam.

I studied a full-year class within a couple of months. I had wasted so much time goofing around the previous year. I took the time to apply myself on top of my other classes and passed the exam early in the new year. Finally, I was assigned to a tenth-grade homeroom.

My Global Studies teacher was promoted to an administrator's position. I took it upon myself to help him with paperwork in the office during lunch break. He became my favorite teacher. Eventually, he was promoted to be the principal. I would still help run errands during my lunch time. He gave me a second chance to shape up rather than shipping out. I was fortunate to get a second chance to get my act together. I am grateful for that wake-up call. I took advantage of the opportunity and improved myself. Through those years of my life, I noticed that I changed when I was hurt for the worse. But, I learned to accept the consequences.

Occasionally, I would babysit our neighbor's four children. I bathed the girl who was twelve. She was autistic. Her brother was two years younger than me. The two younger ones were six and three. Their mother was a nurse and worked late hours. She taught me how to make fried dough and sprinkle sugar for the kids. When she worked late nights, I would sometimes spend the night. I earned cash and would save it to buy what I needed.

The First & The Last

I was back to being studious and not hanging with bad influences. I would mostly hang out with my cousin and her family. I was staying out of trouble. I was never involved in drama or chaos; I kept to myself mostly and was never a part of cliques. I always kept one close friend until they moved or went to a different school.

I had a few encounters with other females who tested me often. However, I never got into arguments or physical fights with anyone until this one time. This was the first and last one. It was early Spring 1990, and I was hanging out with my cousin in a rough part of town. We were minding our business, walking down the street in her biological mother's neighborhood. There was a group of girls walking a distance behind us. One of them shouted that one of us was messing with their man. I knew it was not me. My cousin and I looked at one another, puzzled.

The girls caught up to us. One of them walked in front of us and began walking backward, provoking us. Suddenly, she punched my cousin in the face. My cousin did not react. When she went to sneak up on me, my reflex stopped her hand. I was used to fist-fighting with my siblings. My reflexes were activated. Someone else hit me, and I grabbed her hair. Then, the next thing I know, a girl from behind grabs my arms in a lock. While the girl in front of me scratched up my face, I felt someone try to pull my shorts down. Thank God I had a belt on. It was three girls to one.

My cousin stepped aside and watched me get jumped by three females I had never met. All I could remember was a group of guys behind them cheering them on. Somehow, I got out of the fight, removed my headphones, and handed them to my cousin, who just stood there. I got hit again. I was pulling someone's hair as mine was being pulled.

I don't even know how it was stopped. All I could remember was that my cousin's neighbors came out, yelling at them with baseball bats, and they all ran off. That was my first time being jumped and in a cop's car.

The cop was so upset he said he would like to put them one-on-one with me and let me whoop their behinds. The cop had the girls apologize to me. I found out later from the cop that one of them had a thirty-eight caliber gun in their bag. I was grateful that I did not get shot. I was divinely protected.

Studious Student Struggle

That school year, in the mornings, I had a routine. I would go to the office and deliver the mailing for the teachers in their mailboxes. Sometimes, I made announcements over the P.A. I was still a loner and did not like to go to lunch, so I asked the administrators if they needed help. I would file papers and run errands instead. I was in the halls without a pass, and this time the sentries did not have to chase me. They knew I was volunteering. I made it my business to keep busy and stay out of trouble.

That summer, my baby brother passed away. I was entering my junior year. On the first day of school, I received news that one of my classmates committed suicide. I missed my menstrual period a month later and was pregnant at sixteen. I did not handle my brother's passing too well. My boyfriend had been my distraction from the pain I endured due to losing my baby brother.

Before I found out I was pregnant, I joked around that I would make my parents grandparents, because my two older siblings were married, but none of them had babies. I would joke around, saying I was pregnant. Playing around, I would put a ball under my shirt. Apparently, I manifested my words. Once I was certain I was expecting a baby, I just knew my parents would kill me. Even though they were not as strict anymore, I was still afraid to tell them.

I took it upon myself to make an appointment to view a particular home for young pregnant girls. I filled out the paperwork with my sister just in case my parents flipped. Before I told my parents the news, my mother and I grew closer. She was missing my baby brother, but she never showed her emotions. She would oil and massage my scalp. She would talk about grandchildren's love and what it would be like. I wondered if she knew, but she never spoke about it.

A few months passed, and one day, as she oiled my scalp, I told her I was expecting. She expressed to me that she already knew. She had sensed it from day one. She was not mad, only disappointed. She had just lost her baby boy, so she looked forward to my baby being born. My mother is one strong woman. She is now blind in one eye and has a chronic illness, but she does not allow that to hinder her daily tasks. If you did not know her condition, you would not notice.

She told me we could not tell my dad about the pregnancy yet because of my parents' church religion. My mom made arrangements so that I had to go to a different church before I started showing. I began to visit the Salvation Army Church on Sundays. I made a friend and told her about my pregnancy. There was also a cute little boy by the name of Jonathan who attended the church. On Sunday, he pointed at my stomach and said, "Baby." I was barely showing. I was embarrassed. I said if I had a boy, I would name him Jonathan. During my pregnancy, I had dreams that my brother came back to life. I prayed every night for a healthy baby girl.

I continued my education in my eleventh year and transferred to a school for young mothers. I did not want my peers to know I was pregnant. I worked part-time at the Suny Outreach Program office as an assistant. It was a work program for young mothers. I took an arts and crafts class where I learned how to cross stitch and made my baby a quilt, pillow, and bib. After school, I caught the bus downtown and walked 15 minutes to work. I was filing papers, managing the mail, and answering phones at the office. My boss was amazing, and she spoiled me.

My other boss did not spoil me until one day, he did not bring back one of my cravings that I had asked for. I jokingly told him he would get a stye if he didn't give a pregnant woman what she wanted to eat. The next day, he walked into the office with a stye in his eye. From that day on, he would ask me every day what I wanted to eat. The women in the office would laugh at him whenever he was getting ready to leave for lunch. He made sure he asked me if I wanted anything and brought me food. I was always craving KFC honey barbecue chicken. My female boss would tell me to play a hoax and say that I was in labor, so the men would panic. I always had a playful energy. I had so much fun working there.

When I received my first tax refund check, I bought my first bedroom set. It was a twin-size bed with a dresser. I finally had a new bed. A bed I bought on my own..

It was late February, and my belly was getting bigger. My mother thought it was time to tell my dad. She invited the Salvation Army Church pastor over to share the news with my dad. When the pastor informed him I was expecting, my mother acted like she just found out. I was surprised to see my mother's performance. My dad just shook his leg, looked at my mother, and told her he knew she already knew. Later that day, he left the house because he did not like what he had just heard. He returned, and he and my older brother did not speak to me for at least a month.

It was close to my due date in June. In school, I had to walk up the stairs three times. The next morning, my mucus plug broke. I had no idea what was happening. My mother was working, so I called my baby's grand-mother. She suggested that I stay home. However, I was determined to still attend school despite slight cramps. I had a Doctor's appointment. I was three centimeters dilated.

I was having contractions and went to the hospital that evening, and the nurses made me walk the halls. I was still three centimeters dilated. The doctor said I should go home since the baby was not ready. A little while later, I felt warm fluid trickling down my legs. I was so naive and young. I didn't know my water had broken. I actually said, "Oh shit, I peed on myself. "The nurses rushed me back to the bed and told me my water had broken.

Shortly after, my baby girl was born, and everyone was so in love with her. She was the first grand-baby on both sides. She was spoiled and loved. I did it again during my pregnancy. I wished her to be born on her father's birthday, and she was born on his birthday. I just did not realize he would choose not to celebrate and acknowledge her birthdays. As an adult, I apologized to her for making that wish.

It was my senior year in high school. I had a half-day school schedule. I only had a few classes scheduled in the mornings. I would wake up at five in the morning and prepare myself and my newborn baby girl for the day. Once she turned three months old, she started attending my high school's daycare. It was in the building's basement. We rode the short bus for the mothers and their babies.

Spring came around, and my baby got sick. I took her to the emergency room twice within two weeks. The doctor said she had a viral infection and sent us home. That week was her first birthday. I went back to school with her. The daycare provider told me she had a fever. That day I walked to my sister's house, because she lived near the school. I called 911 and took my baby back to the emergency room. It was her first birthday. This triggered memories of my brother when the ambulance came to our house on the regular. But I was trying my best as a young teen mom to focus on my sick baby girl.

Just imagine my emotions, remembering my baby brother's first birthday brain tumor diagnosis. Now, it was my baby who was sick on her first birthday. It was a flashback moment for me. She was diagnosed with pneumonia and admitted to the hospital on her birthday. She was hospitalized for two weeks. I saw so many children alone in the hospital. One of my elementary friends' babies was one of them. She had four children, and she could not stay by her baby's side. I did not want to leave my baby girl's side. I was fortunate to be able to stay at her bedside. My mom brought me change of clothes and food. My friends also stopped by with food. I would shower while one of them would visit.

On this day, my baby's great-grandmother, who I now call grandmother, was visiting. When the doctor came in and showed me her X-rays, he told me they needed to poke a huge needle with a syringe in her lungs to remove the fluids. He explained that there were side effects. My faith in God was strong. I told them NO to the procedure. I also expressed that I needed them to call my school and inform my teachers that I would not be coming back to school to take my final exams. My teachers exempt me from the final exams. I passed with my final class grade.

While my daughter was in the hospital, I found out I was expecting again. My doctor shook her head as if she was disappointed in me. I was seventeen and pregnant again. I told her that I did give him a condom. I did not enjoy sex. I did it to please him. I felt so ashamed, but I focused on praying for my baby to heal.

It had been two weeks, and my baby girl was discharged on a Friday morning from the hospital the same day I walked the stage and received my high school diploma. Everyone was working, and I did not have a ride home. I called an old friend for a ride. Later that evening, my family and my baby girl's family attended my high school graduation ceremony. I met my baby's great-grandparents when I was pregnant, still wearing the regular clothes I outgrew during my pregnancy. I began to call them grandmother and grandad. And until this present day, I still do. I am blessed to consider them as my grandparents. They unconditionally love my two younger children as if they were their own blood. They have always been very supportive.

My Senior year Grandmother took me shopping for a prom dress. I went to the prom in Dutch (the term meant alone), but I went with a male friend who was not my date. She wanted me to experience my prom. I remember when Grandad got the news that I was expecting his first great-grandchild. Even though he barely knew me, he did not hesitate to take me shopping for maternity clothes at K-Mart. This was new and awkward for me.

My parents could not afford to buy me clothes, but they provided the necessities to maintain for survival. I never had anyone buy me clothes besides my parents. They took me in as their granddaughter; I consider them my grandparents. A few years later, I found out my granddad had the same birthday as my baby brother. Granddad and my third granddaughter, who is his great-great daughter, share the same birthdays well.

My granddad always said I was a 'go-getter kid'. At that time, it did not make sense what he meant. I just did not allow being a young single mother to stop me from chasing my dreams. I innately kept pushing forward. I now understand it for the most part. Granddad is a go-getter himself. He is a veteran. He was run over by a train when he was younger. In his eighties, he was run over by the city bus. Then a few years later, he was run over by another city bus. He survived those tragic accidents. At this present day, as I share my story, Granddad is 100 years old with a sharp mind.

A Maturing Young Adult

The summer after my graduation, I signed up for beauty college. My mother was disappointed in my choices, and she kicked me out. I was seventeen with a one year old and pregnant again. I moved out of my parents' home. My first apartment was in a rundown, creepy old building in a bad area. I was so naïve and gullible. I should have known better, but

I did not. During the walk-through, there were police officers and yellow tape where a victim's body had been found at a murder scene. At that time, it did not click. I just needed a place to live. It was a one-bedroom apartment, and the stove did not work. I was not eating like I ate at my parents.

My boyfriend potentially moved in, but he was never there. He would take the keys with him. I could not leave the apartment. I was practically confined in this place. I soon learned he was selling drugs. The day I found out, I threw his belongings out the window and got my keys back. After living there for one year, I quickly moved out of that place to a better apartment in a decent area.

One day, around the time I was about to move out of my apartment, I was at the laundromat washing clothes. There was a girl that I went to school with there. She was pleasant and spoke briefly about my baby's grandmother. She had a baby boy close in age with my baby girl. My daughter played with him. Twelve years later, we found out the baby boy was my children's older brother. My daughter was not the first grandchild on both sides anymore. It was a small world, after all.

That day, while I was at the laundromat, on the counter, I saw a giveaway for carpet cleaning. I wished I would win. I signed up, and I actually won. I had the carpet steamed and cleaned before moving out. It was a good feeling to win something.

The apartment I moved into was closer to my sister, actually, on the same street. I was happy to be closer to family. I connected with the Young Women's Christian Association of the United States of America (YWCA) and the Catholic Family Center. I had an amazing social worker. She became my surrogate mother. She was always there every time I needed direction when I was distraught. I still check in with her today.

I Knew At A Young Age

Even though I had moved to a better part of town from the first apartment, the double house unit I lived in had dangerous back steps. My landlord threatened me and told me not to report him. At that time, I was not aware of my rights as a tenant. So, I did as he said because I was afraid. He was considered a slum landlord.

During this time, I was unaware my neighbors were using my electricity. I learned of this a year later. I just remember that my bill was always high, and I always wondered how the bills could be so high. I notified my case worker that I could not pay the gas and electric bill. She yelled at me about the bills and put my heat and gas on budget. I tried to explain to her that I was at school all day. She did not want to listen to me and decided that I should receive fifteen dollars every two weeks because of that. It's a good thing I saved my Christmas and birthday money Granddad and Grandmother gave me. It was enough for a young teenager to purchase essentials. Thank God I qualified for school transportation.

Here I was, in the Fall of 1993, an eighteen years old on welfare who had decided to attend beauty college. I caught the city bus to the campus. The city bus did not go to or near the school. So, I had to walk to the building at least fifteen minutes from downtown.

During the freezing cold, snowy days, I cried every day on my way to school. I would tell myself that I would be somebody one day and just imagine it. I was pregnant with a huge belly, wobbling down the street like a penguin. I was so poor I could not afford my uniform. I had to borrow money to pay for it.

I was the only one in class who did not have a hair dryer. During training, we needed a hair dryer to blow dry the ends of the mannequin's hair after cutting it. While every one of my peers had blow dryers, there I was, combing and brushing the hair to air dry it until it was completely dried. My instructor came by to check our mannequin's final results. She pointed out that I was the only one who had done it correctly. My peers were not too pleased since I did not use a blow dryer as they did.

We were taught to be efficient and were instructed to pair up. No one wanted to be my peer, because I had thick, long curly hair. The assistant instructor always had to help my peers with my hair. My instructor would set a timer to see which table would finish first. Those who finished first would go home early. My table always finished first and was excused earlier for efficiency.

Here I was, a single mother, trying to push through my outer circumstances no matter how many were rumoring about me. I did not fit in anywhere. I was a loner, the black sheep in my family. I just knew I was different, but I didn't understand why I was not like the others. My way of thinking and doing things was different from the others. I had my children out of wedlock, embarrassed my family, and was ashamed. But deep down, I knew I wanted to be a cosmetologist and actress since I was eleven. I also wanted to be a model, but I was too short. My height did not stop me from desiring to at least look like one.

At age eleven, my younger brother, two years younger than me, wanted a haircut. He had a crush on a girl and wanted his thick, curly hair to lay straight. My parents could not afford to take him to the barbershop. I took it upon myself and cut his hair. I convinced my brother I had watched the barber cut his hair. Let's just say my dad had to take my brother to the barber to get his haircut corrected.

At age thirteen, I began cutting my hair and receiving compliments. I was cutting my parents' pastor's hair. He was bald on the top. He had me cut his hair for five dollars. My cousin's biological mother liked my mullet haircut, so she paid me five dollars for the same haircut. My dad convinced his barber to let me work at his barbershop at age fifteen. He bought me my first pair of clippers. I have been cutting hair ever since and have mastered it.

My high school offered exploring programs for the youth. I signed up for a career summer program for Cosmetology at Edison Tech. I was always making sure I signed up for opportunities to be better. The participants got a bus pass and paid based on class grade, attendance, and performance. I was so excited when I received my check at the end of the summer program.

During the school year, I signed up for another career program. I attended Tuesday evenings at Shear Ego Cosmetology. My parents were very supportive. I was the only child who had a passion of interest. My mother always signed permission slips for me to explore new endeavors. I never failed a grade, even during my rebellious years of skipping. I did cut it pretty close, but I managed to pass with C's and D's. I knew what I wanted at a young age. It was the drive within me that kept me going.

I also enjoyed being in church plays performing. When I was thirteen years old, I auditioned at an open call. There was an open room full of teenagers. We each went up and performed an improv scene. It was fun to experience. I remember watching television and just imagining my name in the credits. I could see myself performing on television or being one of the hairdressers working onset.

The Lonely Struggle

I was getting closer to my due date. It was the middle of a winter day. I was in cosmetology class and in labor. We would had to stand all day, working on our mannequin. When my instructor saw me sitting down, she always said pregnancy was not a disease. I was having sharp pain. I did not want to draw attention to myself, so I stood and did my breathing exercises quietly.

On my lunch break, I did my breathing in silence and walked up and down six flights of stairs. I knew he was coming, because I walked the stairs with my first pregnancy and gave birth that night. I called my sister and asked if her husband could drop me off at the hospital. Just to set the scene, there was a statewide emergency due to a blizzard that was on its way.

When I arrived at the hospital, the doctor sent me home like always when you are only three centimeters dilated. I was so mad and miserable when I arrived home. I was going to be home alone and give birth. My contractions were one minute apart. My best friend, at the time, was on the phone with me. I was being so stubborn, so she called the ambulance. Because of the storm, it was the worst bumpy ride ever. Keep in mind in labor the whole time. I arrived at the hospital alone and later gave birth to my son.

When my son came home, I quickly began to potty train my nineteen-month-old. I could not afford diapers for one baby, let alone two. I am grateful that she was a quick learner.

One day, I was on the phone with my friend and heard banging on my door and yelling outside. To my surprise, after I had given birth to our second child together, my ex-boyfriend's girlfriend came to my home, banging on the door like a mad woman. I was not a fighter, but I also was not going to allow anyone in to harm me or my children. I placed a skillet with Crisco grease on the stove just in case she managed to come in. I never opened the door. Thank God she left. I told myself I would do my best to be a good mom and protect my babies.

I grew up with my children, with no parental manual for a single teenage mother. I learned along the way. I was considered a baby having a baby and was judged all the time. I did not care because my children were my reason for not giving up. I thanked God every night for them. I had so many obstacles and troubled times. Losing my brother, my babies filled that empty void in my heart. I still missed my baby brother, but now I had a purpose to live for my children.

I was fortunate to return and finish cosmetology school with one thousand credit hours right after my son turned one year old. I even cut my hair off to make it easier for my new peers to work with. I completed the course and graduated that Spring. I was eligible to take the New York State Exam to become a licensed Cosmetologist. I was filled with excitement.

At this time, I had a double umbrella stroller that was a gift from my grandmother. Even though my daughter rode in the stroller, I kept her on a children's leash when she did not want to be in the stroller. I would get ridiculed by strangers, but I did not want to lose my child in public. So, I did not care what they said. It was emotionally hard for me to go in public due to everything we were going through. Not to mention, my daughter's speech was delayed, which made it hard for her to communicate.

One afternoon, I was vacuuming with an old hand-me-down vacuum cleaner. The cord was stiff and hard. It got stuck between my toes. I hopped on one foot from the pain, saying, "Oh, Shit." A few days later, I was on the phone, and my daughter was hopping around on one foot, saying, "Oh, Shit." At the moment, I didn't care. I was so excited my daughter could finally speak. However, it took me a while to un-train her not to say those words, letting her know that only mommy could say them. Eventually, she became a chatterbox. When the kids got a little bit older, Granddad picked them up on the weekends. During one of their visits, my kids said, that Grandad said, "Oh Shit." They told him only Mommy could say those words.

There were times when I could not find a ride to the grocery store. I had to walk one hour one way to the grocery store, pushing a double stroller. I would tie the bags on the stroller and put some underneath. By the time we got home, the bags had torn, and most of my groceries had fallen on the sidewalk. Losing my groceries on the street became normal for me. I remember just crying. At least my babies had their milk and rice cereal.

One time, I was able to afford a cab ride. As I exited the car, my bags tore, and the canned goods fell on the ground. This time, at least, I was a few steps from my door. The cab driver did not even offer to help. I picked up my canned goods and carried them inside. To this day, this is my reason for always requesting double bags at checkout, even though some cashiers seem bothered. They are not the ones who have to worry about broken glass and lost canned goods on the ground.

As you can see, I had many struggling moments, but it did not stop there. I had just received my food stamps and placed them on the dresser. One of my new friends came over. We left my apartment and went to the park. They went back to my apartment to use the bathroom.

A few days later, I found a ride to the grocery store, but could not find my food stamps. I looked all over my small apartment. I kept my apartment clean. I only had a bed, dresser and sofa, so there was no clutter covering up anything. My best friend called me stupid and implied my new friend had stolen my food stamps. I was gullible and did not want to believe it was true. I clearly had not learned my lesson with friends betraying me.

I could not go grocery shopping. The only food in my refrigerator was a bag of broccoli my children's great-grandmother gave me a while back. I did not eat vegetables, only green beans and iceberg lettuce. But that day, I learned to like broccoli enough not to be hungry. I was happy that at least my babies had their milk and rice cereal. I made my bed and lay down to rest.

The next day, my children's family invited me to eat with them at a buffet. I accepted the offer. I was just about to eat my food from the buffet, and my son started having a tantrum, yelling and screaming. I took him to the car to change his diaper and calm him down.

Everyone finished eating and came to the car. I do not think the buffet allowed anyone to take food. I went home starving, still hungry. I was too embarrassed and did not tell anyone about my situation.

Changes For The Better

I finally saved up enough money to buy my first car. It was a three-hundred-dollar car, but it was mine. It got me from point A to point B until it broke down. It was a hoopty that always broke down. I got hustled by the mechanics, because I did not know any better. One day, the engine light came on while driving to the laundromat. This became a wake-up call for me. At this time, my babies were toddlers. I overheard them say, "Awe…, now we got to get in the car with a stranger." I thought, "I can not keep living like this. I have to do better for my children." My poor kids were confused when I told them not to talk to strangers, but there I was, getting in cars with strangers with them, because my car kept breaking down.

That new year, my younger brother drove my kids and me to the used dealership. I used my income tax return and bought my first stick shift car. I was excited about having a better car. On the way home, my brother kept the kids in his car. I was determined to learn to drive a stick shift. I drove my car in first gear all the way home. It jerked the entire time. I kept hearing honking sounds all the way and a peculiar smell. I had no idea what I was doing. But, I was persistent in learning. And in return, I burnt the clutch out.

I had my car fixed, and my friend taught me how to balance the clutch and gas pedal to avoid riding and burning the clutch when shifting gears, especially on hills. I learned how to drive a stick shift within two weeks and mastered it. That was my first time burning a clutch, and I have not burnt one since.

My lease was up on my apartment, and I decided to move to a better one that was subsidized. I was grateful since it was closer to my job. After moving out of the city, I was a licensed cosmetologist who had no luck finding a shop to work at since the first shop I worked at for a short period after graduating from Beauty College. I remembered back when I saw this shop during the bus ride to beauty school every morning. I admired the shop from the outside and wished I could work there someday. My children's cousin worked there, and I was hired for a short period.

I brought a model, performed finger waves, and learned how to sew and glue weaves and do ponytails and braids. However, I did not get a chance to master these techniques. The shop closed down after a few months. The owner was shot and killed.

I could not find a job at a shop, so I took the first offer presented to me to bring in a steady income. I was hired to work as a cashier at a grocery store. My pay started at five dollars and fifteen cents per hour. I learned to be an efficient cashier and acquired great customer service skills. I always observed the managers and front-end runners when there was an error in a transaction, paying close attention to them as they entered the override codes on the register with a key. I was one of the top cashiers, and my till was always even. I made sure I counted the money three times before handing it to the customer. I worked most holidays for time and a half pay, except Christmas Day and Kwanza. I would only use my vacation time once a year. But for the most part, I would cash in my vacation hours.

I was hired as a part-time employee, working full-time hours, and getting recognition for being the Employee of the Month quite often. Each time, I requested a raise. For the most part, they would honor it for me. That was huge earnings for me, coming from a ground-zero poor girl.

I was very trustworthy. The managers allowed me to keep my coat and purse in their office, because I was polite, pleasant, and one of the best employees. When I was being considered for promotion, I heard that several department managers wanted me to work in their departments. I knew each one of their names, so I always greeted them. I was soon promoted to the Deli department.

Back to the stick shift car. It kept breaking down, not the clutch. A mechanic showed me that spark plugs were missing. I bought another used car for two hundred dollars to get me to work. It also kept breaking down. I was tired of walking long distances to and from work in bad weather. I applied for my first loan with the credit union to build my credit to purchase a reliable car. I fixed the car I bought for two hundred, sold it for three hundred, and traded in my stick shift car for my first brand new car. It only had twenty miles on the odometer, and it was, of course, a five-speed stick shift.

I did not have enough credit, but they worked with me. Not the best deal on APR, twenty-four percent. Now I know that was awfully high interest. But, I did not care about the payments. I just wanted to finally drive with my children without worrying about my car breaking down and flagging down strangers for a ride.

Many nah-sayers tried to convince me not to purchase a new car, a Jeep. They tried to scare me by saying that Jeeps would flip. But, I decided I was getting what I wanted on my own. I didn't care what they thought. They were not the ones who had to walk one hour one way to work, during rainy thunderstorms days or cold winter snow days. Or take a chance putting their babies and their lives in a stranger's car.

What kept me pushing to get a new car was when I reflected on a day when the weather was so bad, and I had to walk home. And by the time I got there, I was covered in snow, a walking snowwoman. I was tired of walking in thunderstorms for one hour one way or during winter storm days just to go to work. Keep in mind, I was afraid of lightning and thunderstorms. I was just happy that I had the opportunity to make a change in my life.

I was excited to drive my Jeep off the lot with only twenty-four miles on it. It was brand new. I loved my Jeep. It had a four-wheel drive, and was able to drive out of my parking spot in the snow. However, an old friend crashed and totaled it six years later. And, guess what. It did not flip like everyone was suggesting it would. That was my first new car, and so far, I have not purchased a brand-new one since.

As things unfolded for the better, I purchased my children their first new bunk bed from Fingerhut Catalog. They offered a payment plan. When it arrived, I stayed up all night and put it together all by myself. I will admit I did not read the directions; it looked self-explanatory. After I built it, I glanced at the directions. It required two people to build this full-size bunk bed: full size at the bottom and twin on top. But, I managed to do it on my own.

Things were going slightly better for us. I was able to start enjoying my life as a young single mother and spend time with my friends. My children would spend time with my parents and grandparents during the weekends.

During the holidays, I would buy my children extra toys from the Dollar Tree store so that they could open a lot of presents. I remembered how my cousin and her biological sister would open a lot of presents on Christmas Day, and my siblings and I only had one. I never wanted my children to experience what I had experienced. I bought them a lot of presents. I also made sure my children wore nice clothes so their peers would not tease them.

Blessings Connected Us

Before I was promoted to the Deli department, many customers preferred my register line for checkout. After my promotion, they would still come by and look for me. One day, one of my customers, a foster mother I admired for loving all the children that came to her home, came in with a new baby. She stopped by to show him to me. I stepped out of the Deli counter and asked his name. He was my friend's baby boy. His mother was one of my closest friends. She had placed him in temporary foster care. She was an amazing young mother with two children. Her firstborn had a disability.

We both were pregnant at sixteen, and she did everything possible for her babies. I teased her that she would have the baby on her oldest son's birthday. She was due the same month and gave birth on that day. I did it again. I spoke it into existence, not knowing the power behind it. I cried and picked him up, squeezed and kissed him. My friend missed her baby boy and went to get him back. She is a phenomenal mother.

She also lived in the city thirty minutes away. What a coincidence this was. It was crazy to me how everyone I came in contact with was connected to someone I knew.

While working in the Deli department, I learned to roll dough for pizza and used a recipe book to cook sauces for the sweet and spicy chicken wings, chicken, and broccoli. If I was cleaning for the closing of the Deli and a customer came by, I would still service them. I was there to serve the customers.

Here are a few more happenings like this in my life. While working as a cosmetologist, I had a female client in my chair. She had a cute little girl. I complimented her daughter and said she reminded me of my ex-boyfriend. She asked me his name. She told me that he was her father. Again, what were the odds on that? Meeting people that I was connected to in some way happened regularly.

Another client of mine was a cop. He always requested me. Later, I found out he was my friend's older brother. I never met him, only heard about him. I continued to cut his hair until he moved to a different state.

Back to the Deli. It had been two years since I had worked in the Deli department. While working, I injured my right wrist and did not complain. The next day, I came to work, but I could not carry anything that weighed more than five pounds. The Deli manager was upset and seemed annoyed with me, because I could not work as productively as I used to. I eventually had to go to therapy.

I also had a hard time driving my car since it was a standard shift. It would have worked fine if the driver's seat was on the right side, like in other countries. I still drove my car and struggled to shift with my injured hand. Even though it was challenging, I managed that obstacle just as I have others.

Life was so much better than before, but deep down, I was not happy. I wanted more. I took a leap of faith and applied for a stylist position at a shop. They called me in for an interview, and I was hired. On my first day, the manager was fired, and the acting manager had no idea I was a new employee. When she found out, they proceeded with my orientation process as a new stylist.

I was trained and enjoyed cutting hair. I learned new hair-cutting techniques, used the customer service skills I learned while working at the grocery store, and did my best with my performance.

My co-workers would argue with each other in every monthly meeting.

I would always ask to be dismissed since I was never involved in the drama. I did my best to avoid the shop's drama. I remained diligent in my position, and I was awarded Employee of the Year.

It was mandatory for every stylist to work from open to close on the "Back to School" day. The manager announced that whoever had the most haircuts would win a prize. I had already been trained to be efficient while attending the beauty college and as a cashier. I was confident in winning. By the end of my 12-hour shift, I had serviced fifty clients. I won a pair of clipper blades for my Oster clippers.

After working in heels at the salon all day, I would be so exhausted. So, I cut back on my hours at the Deli department. Soon after, I decided to attend community college. I would work at the Deli in the morning, go home, take a fifteen-minute nap between shifts and classes, and then go to the shop. That semester, I pulled a 4.0.

The next semester, I was in the early stage of my third pregnancy. I had morning sickness throughout the day. I was tired, not focused, and did poorly that semester. I got passing grades, and as a result, my GPA dropped. I was not applying myself. Therefore, I did not register for the spring semester.

I quit working at the shop and the grocery store, because I started spotting. I did not want to lose my baby. My baby's health was my priority, but I also had to figure out how to survive. My best friend and I agreed that I would let her use my credit cards, and she would give me the cash for her spending. Therefore, I could pay bills. When she was finishing her last year in college, she stopped working to focus on school. We worked it out again. This time, I gave her the cash and used her credit card for the equivalent amount I spent.

Standing Up for Myself & Others

When my daughter turned six months old, I returned to work at the shop. Fortunately, I left in good standing with the district manager. My mother was no longer working, so she was able to watch her. Once again, we moved to a better neighborhood and into a nice townhouse. My older kids each had their own room.

The district manager assigned me to a different salon. I did not mind because it was closer to my townhouse. Within a few weeks, the store manager was terminated. The region manager took over the shop. I watched the region manager when she was on the computer, and I asked one hundred questions. She did not mind giving me the answers and suggested I apply for the manager position. Ten other stylists applied, and I was fortunate to get the position.

There was a major transition in effect. My training was brief, and I had to figure it out on my own. I compared it to motherhood. I had to weed out the ones trying to hinder me as the new manager. When I started as a stylist, the assistant manager applied for the same position. It did not sit well with her that I was the new stylist at that location and now her boss. I kept those who were on board with this new transition. I hired and trained new employees and selected my assistant managers.

I knew that If I wanted my employees to follow my expectations, I also had to meet those expectations. I placed expectations and tried my best to be fair. I learned a lot along the way. Sometimes, I forgot I was the manager because I never had a power trip. I tried to make it a fun working environment and set boundaries. We did not have drama. I did not tolerate it.

One Saturday, I had a female client who was slightly older than I was. As I was cutting her hair, she had a seizure and fell off the chair. I called 911. That same day, a little boy ran out of the shop and into the phone booth.

His forehead was injured and bleeding. I had to call 911 again. When I closed out the drawer for the day, it was 666. As I drove to my parents, an older woman was driving on the wrong side of the road. She was coming directly towards me. I was able to dodge her car. Thankfully, we were all safe. She did not collide with anyone. I was overwhelmed and grateful to be alive. I looked up the meaning of 666. I am not sure where I found it, but it said that seeing 666 tells you to pay closer attention to any fixation you currently have on earthly problems and details. And that is exactly what I did.

In my first year in management, I was recognized as the Manager of the year. I learned how to record stats and build my schedule. I mastered how to keep everyone happy. My employees were reaching their sales goals and earning more than the base scale, depending on how many haircuts they had per hour. Everyone in my shop was happy. We had an algorithm. The district manager was pleased with my performance.

We had a managers' conference in Orlando, Florida. That was an experience in itself. I experienced racism with a few of my fellow co-workers. I was the only non-caucasian, and they were very bold about it. It is sad to say that because of my outer appearance, I have experienced racism. I have experienced racism from my own in my Hispanic community and black and white communities. During this time in my life, my mindset was different. I was tired of being bullied and mistreated. So, I learned to stand up for myself.

That week was interesting. During the day, we attended seminars. There was a speaker who welcomed us. He began by announcing winners for a brand new pair of Hikari shears. They were expensive. I sat in my seat and thought to myself, "I bet he says my name." Within five minutes, he was struggling with the pronunciation. I knew it was me, and it was me. I felt good about winning an expensive pair of shears. I was timid to go up and receive my shears. There were hundreds of managers in the auditorium from all over.

I shared a hotel room with my supervisor. When we got back to the room, she pointed out to me that she was surprised at how timid I was. She assumed I was not based on how I dressed and carried myself. I was surprised she saw me in this manner.

During one of the sessions, a motivational speaker talked about finances and formulas. I was able to follow along because I was familiar with it. My supervisor was not able to comprehend. I assisted her in understanding. She was surprised that I was familiar with problem-solving and mathematics. As you know, I have experienced many problems and learned a lot about people and how to deal with them.

When I returned to my shop, it was back to work. My employees began to feud with each other. They would call me on my days off about walk-ins and who would receive credit for other clients' product purchases. One stylist would cut the client's hair, and another stylist would ring up the customer and get credit for the sale. To avoid the drama, I decided who clocked in first that day, including me, would be the first to get the walk-ins, then next in rotation to avoid conflict. I was fair with my employees. The last time I visited, I noticed the cards on the front end as I had paced them while managing the store. This practice was still in place after I resigned. I made a difference, and I was proud of it.

We got along for the most part, because they knew I did not do drama. I would instead have them all meet up at a restaurant to discuss their issues, and they got paid for their time.

One night, we were celebrating Christmas, and a few of the girls drank too much. My assistant manager and I were the only ones sober. We had to be strategic to make sure everyone got home safely. We each drove a car with the girls and dropped them off at one location. Then, we both got in one car to drive back to the restaurant to bring each car to one place.

They were all friends outside of work. I knew they all needed to spend the night at the same house. It was a long and interesting night driving back and forth, but we finally had the three cars at the house. I was grateful that my assistant manager was there to assist me. As a manager, it did not sit well with me if any of my employees drove home intoxicated. I felt responsible and wanted them to be safe.

I was a twenty-seven years old single mother with three children, managing a shop. I was unhappy in my situation even though I managed for three years and received manager of the year. I wanted and needed change.

The Big Move

After my vacation in Jamaica, within less than two months, I decided to move to Florida. My cousin, who lived in Florida, convinced me to move. At first, I was reluctant because I had security with my mother watching my children while I worked. However, my cousin was very persuasive. She said she would help me with my children while I worked. I applied for a three-bedroom apartment and was approved. The apartment was move-in ready.

I flew to Florida to sign my lease. I informed my supervisor that I was moving, and she referred me to another Florida shop manager. I returned to Rochester confident with a job lined up and a nice three-bedroom. This would be my first time having my own bathroom. It was all settled: a new job, a new apartment, and my children would be with my cousin while I worked. Everything was lined up for this major transition. I calculated gas, mileage, and so forth. Everyone thought I was crazy for making an impulsive move. The funny thing is, those same people, at least a few, moved out of Rochester a few years after I did.

One day before the big move, my cousin called and told me she could not watch my children while I worked because she had to work. I was in shock. However, I could not be upset with her. I was calm, but the tears just fell down my face. I had resigned from my job and had not renewed my lease. I was upset with myself for trusting my cousin's words. I should have known better. I always have experienced disappointments when I put my trust in others.

I called my mother, crying. My mother told me that out of all her kids, I was the only one who said I would do something and always did it. I had no idea my mom observed me in this manner. I could not disappoint her. And, I had signed a lease, and a job was waiting for me.

That night, I dreamed of God with a small being with wings and an illuminated light. They said to go to Florida. I woke up peacefully and proceeded as planned. In the fall of 2003, I moved to Florida. I made calls to find out how to navigate around the city. Back then, there was no GPS. I had to figure my way around this new town. I learned my way from the people who lived there and knew how to get to work from several directions.

Let me backtrack a little and tell you about my experience with my supervisor when I resigned from my manager position. She confessed that she liked having me as a manager. However, she was intimidated by me, because she thought I was smarter than her. She felt relieved that I was leaving.

She did not know that I understood the financial part during the managers' conference in Orlando because I took a financial class in college. However, I did not take her confession as a compliment after experiencing racism among the other managers. I was the first non-white manager in that district. I learned and experienced so much while keeping my management position until I resigned. I now had the confidence to move on.

I was scheduled to start my job as soon as I moved to Florida. So, the first thing I did was get my children registered for school. I could not work full-time as I imagined I would. I did not have childcare for my two-year-old baby. After a month, I finally found child care, but my baby kept getting sick. This was her first time around other children besides our family. She would feel better and then be sick again the following week. This was a challenging time for me.

My new employer informed me that my Cosmetology license was invalid in Florida. I was unaware of that part when I decided to move. It was a rude awakening for me. I did not have time to go to school. I had bills to pay and had to provide for my children. Florida and New York licenses did not reciprocate each other. I had to go back to cosmetology school for two hundred hours to receive a Cosmetologist license in Florida. My New York State Cosmetology License was for one thousand hours, and Florida State required twelve hundred hours. I was devastated; I needed to work. We were eating mayonnaise sandwiches. I had so many moments of breaking down. I had saved up my income tax return, so I had enough to pay rent.

During this time, I received a check for five hundred dollars. Until this day, I did not know who it came from. It was written out to me and was a business check. I thought my old electric company was paying me back because they found out my neighbor was stealing my gas and electricity. However, I never found out who the check was from. I was grateful. I was struggling again, but this time, my kids were older.

One day, my apartment complex had an event. They were selling pizza. My kids wanted some. I found spare change, but I was short. I asked the lady if I could run to my apartment for the rest. My kids and I went through my stuff for spare change. My son ran back to pay off the remaining balance. I was happy my kids were happy.

During my transitional, challenging period, I had a moment where I could not control my emotions. My babies just cried with me. They hugged me as I curled up on the floor. My oldest daughter came to my room and told her younger brother and baby sister to leave me. She facilitated them to leave my room and closed the door behind her. She was so mature. I made a lot of mistakes, and I learned along the way. I realized I had to do better. Transitioning was not as easy as it seemed.

I began working part-time as a receptionist at another shop until I could get my hours to receive my Florida cosmetology license. I was grateful that it was closer to my apartment.

In the summer, my kids were too young to stay home alone: eleven, ten, and two years old. I went to The Beauty College administrator, who was dismissive and gave me an assessment. I scored eighty percent. She informed me that I needed to score higher and I would have to take five hundred hours in the school. Most of the questions were the same questions from the exam I took eight years prior.

Going to school required eight hours days, Monday through Friday. I would not have time to work or spend time with my children. After finding out this information, the receptionist saw me in tears. She pulled me to the side and whispered to me another option. She suggested I go to Barnes & Noble, purchase the exam booklet, and challenge the board. I drove to Barnes & Noble that day and bought the booklet as she suggested. I studied daily, even at the gym on the elliptical, reading the questions and answers. I was determined to pass the exam and work.

One of my co-workers had the CD for the exam and lent it to me. It was right on time, just when I needed it. It allowed me to practice taking the exam as many times as I needed with the results. I quizzed myself daily until I scored one hundred. I kept taking the practice exam and scoring one hundred percent. I intended to pass the exam and work as a Florida Cosmetologist.

In February 2004, I scheduled to take my state board exam. It was a thirty-minute drive. I walked into a professional building and challenged the state board. I was the only one taking the exam that day. They facilitated me to the exam room. I was so confident with Theory Part One. It was science, anatomy, and chemistry. I knew every layer in the skin, nail, hair follicle, radius finger, etc. I knew all the answers like the back of my hand. I was confident and got all of them correctly.

The second part of the exam was Practical. In New York State, the practical exam required a live model. I closed my eyes and prayed to God. None of the questions seemed familiar. However, I knew the definitions of a lot of the main words. I used common sense with the questions. For example, one of the questions that stood out was a scenario about baking soda cut greases. That was easy to answer. I continued with the exam, trusting I was answering them when I recognized a technical word. I was finally done with my exam.

I walked back to the receptionist to let her know. I was certain I passed Part One. I was not quite certain about passing Part Two. I asked her when I would get my exam results. She was tactful and responded, "Now." She looks at the results and puts one thumb up, then a second time, thumb up. I could not believe I had passed The Practical Exam. I challenged the state board and was now a Florida Cosmetologist without taking the five hundred hours course, and it also costs less. Immediately, I began working as I had originally planned.

At the end of the school year, we drove to Rochester using printed MapQuest directions. This was my first time driving alone long distance with my children since we moved to Florida. We left early in the morning. My oldest stayed up with me while the two young ones slept. It was as if I had told them to sleep, but I hadn't.

During the trip, I got tired and pulled into a McDonald's parking lot. My younger ones woke up, and my oldest was tired. I promised my baby girl ice cream if she would be quiet while we rested. When I woke up from my nap, my baby girl was so quiet. She reminded me to get her ice cream.

When we reached New York State, I got off an exit to get gas. It was a creepy place, gas stations much like they were in the eighties. The man at the front was creepy. It reminded me of a Scooby Doo episode. My children thought it was creepy as well. There was heavy fog, and the visibility was poor. After getting gas, I quickly grabbed my Bible and prayed for guidance. As I drove on the 90 East, I followed a vehicle with hazard lights on with caution until the fog cleared up.

When we finally reached Rochester, the men in my family scolded me and told me never to drive like that again. I was anxious to get home to see everyone. On my MapQuest directions, the drive from Florida to New York was nineteen hours and forty minutes. We were on the road for twenty-four hours with my resting stop. My fingers were cramped from holding on to the steering wheel. When I finally layed on a bed, I and slept like a baby. I have never driven like that since.

When I returned to Florida, I was working and had childcare. Things were aligning for me. However, my baby was still getting sick. As I mentioned before, this was her first time in public daycare. I began to work at another franchise shop and found a private babysitter. I was back on track once again. Then, the babysitter moved. This happened for the first two years like a yo-yo. I had a job, but no babysitter. I had experienced working at so many different jobs compared to the few jobs I had back home.

I couldn't wait until my eleven year old was twelve so she could babysit legally while I worked during the summertime. I had been working at two different shops on a seven day schedule.

The time came, and I decided to walk into a private shop in Pine Hills. It was considered the hood area. The female owner only hired barbers. At the time, she had male barbers. She gave me the rundown and hired me on the spot. I appreciated her for that. While working there, I learned how to bald fade and shape up, a different terminology for the same style haircuts compared to northern terms.

I kept my hair braided, because it was hot. Everyone thought I favored Alicia Keys. I would bring my kids to the shop on Saturdays, because I did not have anyone to watch them for me.

Soon, it was time to move on. I went to an interview at a barbershop nearby. It was like working at the DMV, with clients grabbing a ticket. I felt so bad, since I could not remember faces. It was like an assembly line. I was always tired, working Monday through Saturday. Within the three years of living there, I worked at least eight or more shops until I found the right one.

Things got better as the kids got older. Things were finally lining up for me. My daughter was old enough to stay home with the kids. By that time, I was working at a busy shop with at least twenty stylists. I had admired this shop from the outside when I first moved to Florida, wishing I could work there.

One stormy day, my daughter called me and said my baby girl was crying, scared of the thunder. I was fifteen minutes away. I told my co-workers what was happening in case anyone asked where I was. I left the shop and drove home quickly in the rain to comfort my baby girl. When I returned to the shop, my manager apparently realized I was not there. I told her I was in the bathroom.

Eventually, I quit that shop, because the assistant manager had a power trip. It did not sit well with me. I was a manager of a shop and knew to respect my employees. I had more jobs in Florida than I did back home.

Florida had intense storms. I was not fond of hurricanes either. I was so stressed about Hurricane Ivan coming as predicted. I drove to Atlanta and stayed with my children's aunt. We call each other sisters. We stayed with her for a week or so.

When I returned to Florida, I applied at a salon and started working that week. A former co-worker from one of the previous shops worked there as well. We worked at several different shops together. I loved working at this shop. They were not about drama life. My workers were the best to work with.

However, it was uncomfortable when I was scheduled to work alone with the manager. She was married and having an affair with the shop owner. The manager would smile and greet the shop owner's wife after being intimate with her husband in the office. My station was next to the office, and the walls were thin. It was awkward and uncomfortable. My co-workers knew about it. Nevertheless, I hung in there for a short while.

My co-workers were fun to work with and were shocked when I told them I went to bars and comedy clubs alone. Yes, I finally had a babysitter. I carried a pocket knife in my bra; I was cautious. Back then, they did not search anyone before entering a bar or club. I learned to enjoy my own company. My co-workers invited me to go out with them as well. We would all hang out and have fun; no female drama.

That summer, I planned to celebrate my oldest and younger daughter's birthdays with family and friends back in Rochester. This time, I planned to stop in West Virginia to rest. It was a Friday morning, and I was ready and packed to head out. I woke up with a stiff, sore neck. I know I am a risk- taker, but it's only because I know God is carrying me through it all. We packed the car and started our trip. I proceeded to drive with a pillow behind my head. A state trooper drove past me, looking at me strangely. He continued in his lane as I continued driving.

When we stopped in West Virginia, we checked into a motel. The following morning, I could not move my neck at all. I was on the floor, crying due to the pain. My children were trying to help me. I finally felt good enough to continue my drive.

I told my best friend about my neck pain when I reached Rochester. I still had to drive twenty hours that Sunday back to Florida. I had to be back to work on that Monday. She suggested I go to Gold's Gym and get a massage. Her friend spoke highly about a massage therapist at this location. That was my first time getting a massage. My masseuse was a dark, handsome, muscular man. I was not comfortable, so I did not take off my clothes. As he began to rub my shoulder, he asked me if I would like my gluteus maximus massaged. I told him no, only to massage my upper body to help alleviate my neck pain. I only wanted him to focus on my neck. He focused on my shoulder blades.

Instantly, my pain disappeared. I was able to move my neck. I told my best friend about my experience; she couldn't believe I turned down the full-body massage. I felt better, and that was my intention. Apparently, I slept on too many pillows. Since then, I have no longer slept on more than two pillows.

One day after returning to Florida, while at work, a few stylists and I talked about life and its struggles. One co-worker suggested I read Don't Sweat the Small Stuff by Richard Carlson. My client told me he was a motivational speaker and also suggested that I should read "The Magic Of Believing by Claude M. Bristol, Think and Grow Rich by Napoleon Hill, and How To Win Friends and Influence People by Dale Carnegie. He suggested I read in that order and reread every year.

Well, I took his suggestions. I read the books and realized I had been using my innate gifts since I was a child. I believe he was sent there to deliver that message to me. Nothing happens by coincidence.

Now you see why I enjoyed my career so much. One of my clients offered me my first speaking role for a commercial. I accepted, and I filmed a few times with him.

The Weather Moved Us

My daughter was not happy, and complained about Florida's heat. And, I could not take the hurricanes. They were touching down weekend after weekend. I did love Florida; the people were amazing, and I was happy, and I finally had somewhat of a balance in my life. It took me almost three years to get there. However, the hurricanes were just too overwhelming for me. We experienced power outages with no water for two weeks in over 100-degree weather. But, we survived it. I truly loved Florida, but the hurricanes were too much for us to bear.

While living in Florida, I began my spiritual journey; my faith in God was stronger. I had so many obstacles and a lot of turbulence. But, I also experienced a lot of greatness. When I read The Magic of Believing, I realized I did some of those exercises independently as a child without reading the book. It was my innate wisdom as a young girl. I was unaware of the Power of Thoughts manifesting until I read this book. I was on the right path.

I decided that if I made it happen in Florida, on my own, and survived hurricanes and life's storms with three kids, then I could go anywhere and do it even better. I was beyond confident and did it again. There were a lot of naysayers who thought I was crazy for moving around with kids on my own. But deep down, I knew I wanted better. I didn't understand it with clarity, but I was listening to something deep within myself. I decided to move to North Carolina halfway back north.

I drove to North Carolina with the set intention of finding a job and a place to live. I stayed with my children's cousin. She took me to the barbershop where she went for her cuts. They offered me a position, and I accepted. I also went to two other shops and several leasing properties.

That night, I dreamt of a gold coin falling from the sky with my full name on it. I woke up feeling great. I had one more leasing property to check out. The leasing office was closed for lunch. I drove around the corner to a gas station. Along the way, I saw one of the franchise shops I worked for. I thought this was a sign, so I went in and spoke with the manager. I gave her my resume, and I was hired as a stylist.

I headed back to Florida, feeling accomplished. I had a place to live and two jobs. Now, looking back, it sounds like peaches and cream. When we moved to North Carolina in the Fall of 2006, I ensured my kids were in school.

I started working on a Friday and had one client. I was disappointed. I was used to not taking a break on Fridays due to being busy cutting hair all day. I needed to earn an income to provide. That day, I walked into another shop in my area. They offered me a position, and I accepted. The next week, I was in orientation for the franchise shop. The manager was so busy that I ended up training their new employee. They hired me because my regional manager from New York was the store's regional manager. Plus, my resume was well polished with so much experience. I was confident in my performance. I had faith, and I believed in myself. I gave my resignation to the previous shop, even though I only worked one day.

Working at the busier shop, I continued to work as an established barber and built my clientele. I went to bartending school and began working with a catering company for a short time. During this time, my daughter was being bullied, and my workplace was far away. So, I impulsively chose the first affordable builder to build a home in a safe area closer to my workplace for me and my children.

New Place, New Space

I had our first home built in 2007. My children picked everything out in the showroom. I promised my kids they would each have their own room, and we would have a garden. I kept my word. I chose to create a space for myself with no judgment, removing all my veils. This is how I became the woman that I am today. Through the pain and struggles, I overcame each one. It became the norm for me when I realized how the norm was affecting me. I could not live a fulfilled life because I created several blockages with my scarcity mindset.

I understood how to unblock the blockages to set myself free and live joyously without monetary concerns. As a young single mother, I felt accomplished. I was setting intentions and completing them. I had to be a better role model for my children. So, they can see that I never allowed my outer circumstances to victimize me. I was learning along the way with my children, watching my every move. I began to take control to become victorious and believe in miracles.

Psalms 23:4 (NIV)

"Even though I walk through the darkest valley, I will fear no evil, for you are with me; your rod and your staff, they comfort me."

Day 

Obtaining My Power

I sequestered myself from society and became a hermit. Being home alone became tiring. I decided to take a trip to Aruba and booked an excursion tour to Arikok National Park. The tour was on a hot day. I drank a lot of water to stay hydrated and constantly went to the restroom during the tour.

After one of my bathroom trips, I didn't see the tour guy or the other tourists. I tried to use the GPS on my iPhone, but it was not picking up a signal. I was not able to reach anyone for assistance in directions. Thankfully, I remembered how to get back to the tour van. At least, I thought I did. I found myself going around in circles.

I was determined to find the nearest tower to get a signal. However, I could not seem to find a tower or anyone. I took a deep breath and exhaled. As I continued walking, hoping to find my tour group, I found myself standing near a beautiful botanical garden. It was filled with distinguished floral vines throughout the pathway. Straight ahead, I saw an illuminating light. I began to walk towards it.

As I was walking, I glanced down. I noticed that the ground was made of a gold texture, and I was now barefoot. The rays of the sun were reflecting on the ground. It was as if I was in a different world. I knew that I could not have been hallucinating. I wondered if the heat could have affected my mind in this way. I just kept on going. I felt this nice and warm sensation beneath my feet with each step I took. I was not afraid. I felt this peaceful feeling. The smell of the air was pristine. I was in paradise.

As I walked closer toward the light beaming so bright, I saw a majestic archway. I walked through and arrived at a celestial palace. The architecture of the place was indescribable. I noticed the walls were made of crystalline, gold, and diamond. The windows were made of clear crystal quartz. I was captivated by this euphoric place. I began to feel so light, as if I were floating in the air. However, my feet were still on the ground. I just felt lighter. I was feeling overjoyed.

I heard this voice say, "Today is a day to celebrate." I looked around to see where the voice came from. White angels with golden halos floated in the sky, with beautiful wings flapping away. My ancestors were gathered in the open court. Every being was full of love and joy. I could feel their love. Something was being placed on my head. It was The Divine placing a golden crown with emeralds on my head. I was astounded and looked up at him. His eyes lit up as he looked into my eyes like a proud parent with their toddler taking the first steps. He says to me, "There, now, my child. You are ready to finally sit back on your throne."

The throne was made of rose quartz, and the arms were detailed carved designs. The seat was soft as silk. I sat up straight with my crown on my head and my arms on my throne. The throne was a perfect fit for my petite stature, as if it was designed just for me.

The Divine: This is your birthright.

Me: My birthright? I'm from a royal bloodline? (I was lost and confused.)

The Divine: Of course, my child. You are my child. Why would you not be royal blood? You were so caught up in your flesh and the worldly things, you managed to dethrone yourself. You were walking blindfolded for quite some time. But, now you have finally awakened and understand who you truly are and your reason for being in this lifetime. We are all so overjoyed with happiness to watch you complete each cycle. You have a better under-standing of each experience as a lesson. Deep down, you always knew who you were. That is why we always kept you alone most of the time. But, we were very close to you every step of the way! We have sent you so many angels to help you through your journey. We also had to interfere and disturb your world. There were times that you did not pay attention to signs to move on from the situation. You are a stubborn one, but that's why you were the chosen one. Your ancestors chose you to break the generational curses. You have done the work and still have more to complete. It is your time to begin to co-create greatness on Earth. Continue to operate from love and spread love to others. As you already know, you vibrate higher with love. You have healed so many with just a smile gesture and your silly personality. You played small for too long. You were never created to be small. You were comfortable and became complacent for too long. You have learned to unlearn the old ways and relearn new ways. Every time you fell, you kept getting up. You persevered no matter what circumstance you endured. It was hard for us to watch. We wanted to reach out and pick you up and comfort you, but we knew you could do it. Each time you got up, you were stronger. You kept asking for strength. We gave you several situations to help you activate your strength. You always had it within you. Each day, in every way, you just become better and better with time. I know you feel that you have lived a hard life and always felt like you were alone. But from here on, you will live abundantly blissfully because you made one simple change, an attitude of gratitude. We are all so proud of you. You chose to go within and let go of the outer circumstances. You're on your path of becoming extraordinary! Your outer circumstances do not define who you are. The true spiritual being inside you reflects your true world."

There I was, ready to shine with the Divine! It was like a light switch turning on the lights. I took my power back and claimed my inheritance. I was feeling so joyful and free. Then, I heard my alarm go off. I reached over to my nightstand to turn off the buzzing sound. As I lay in my bed, I thanked

God for everything he has done for me and continues to do for me.

Earthly Angels

Financial, Chauffeur & Encouraging Angels

I began to reflect on many past obstacles when earth angels came my way. One of these obstacles happened during a chaotic period in my life. It was a cold Sunday winter day in Rochester, New York. I had two broken -down cars, a.k.a. Hoopties. I was grateful that my oldest brother came by to see if he could help me figure out one of the car's problems.

I was so broke. I did not have a dime to my name. He gave me ten dollars. That was a lot of money for me. I was grateful for the blessing. I put it in my pocket. I was so emotional and a poor lost soul during this time. I was living from resentment, fear, and pain.

My daughter was three years old then, and my son was two. Their father's mom picked us up to visit him while he was in the hospital. He and I were no longer together. So, during the visit, I made sure I remained cordial.

My son asked for a drink. He and I went to the lounge to see if they had a vending machine. A group of people looked like they were coming from church. I asked them if anyone had change for the ten dollars. One gentleman pulled his wallet out and looked through it. He only had a couple of dollar bills. He turned to the people in his group and asked them. Everyone looked in their purses and wallets, but no one had the exact amount. They each put what they had together to the equivalent of ten dollars, and I gave the gentleman my ten-dollar bill. I thanked them all and went to the vending machine to purchase my son's drink.

We went back to the room. As my son was playing on the floor, he picked something up. He handed it to me and said out loud, "Mommy, your picture." It was the Christmas picture of me and the kids I had given to them. My face had been cut out of the picture. I was so hurt. I cried, spoke my mind, and ran out with my kids. I called everyone I could think of to pick us up and take us home. I had no luck. I felt so alone.

We walked to the bus stop. As I was standing crying, a man was standing nearby. Soon, the bus had arrived at the stop. I got on the bus with my babies and immediately asked the bus driver if there was a bus that went to my side of town. She looked at me, and her response was no. We sat down, and I cried during the bus ride. We arrived downtown. The bus driver looked at me and told me to come with her. She got off the bus, walked across the street, and opened the doors of a white 4-door car. I proceeded to follow her. She told me to get in her car. And said to me, "I'm taking you home."

My kids fell asleep during the long car ride. When we arrived home, she helped me carry them to our apartment. She asked if I had a Bible. I brought out my Bible, and she opened it to Psalms 121. I told her my mom made sure I memorized this psalm as a young girl. I thanked her for her kindness. I do not remember her name or if she told me. I was in such an emotional state. What were the odds that this earth angel's shift was ending and she would be available to drive my children and me back home?

She didn't have to drive me home, but she did. I lived in a subsidized apartment complex outside the city. I was so grateful for the ride, because we were far from the house. And especially because it was during the winter season. The way this uneventful moment played out as if it was orchestrated. If my brother had not given me the ten dollars, if my son had not wanted a drink, and if the nice people in the lounge room had not given me change, I would not have had the accurate bus fair to ride the bus that evening. I also considered those people earth angels.

During that time of my life, I worked as a cashier. A few months after this awful circumstance occurred, I was at work, and a man asked me, "Are you good now?" I looked at him. He was the man at the bus stop. He walked by the next register with groceries and stopped to speak to me. I was in shock. The hospital was on the other side of town. What a coincidence! He was in my neck of the woods. At this time, I wasn't aware of earth angels. These are the times that I remember vividly. As you read, you will see that I had more occasions of being served by and being an earth angel.

Assisting Angels

I have had the opportunity to experience assisting angels as well. I could only afford to purchase train tickets during my first trip out of town with my babies. Just imagine, this was an adventure for a single young mother with two toddlers earning five dollars and fifteen cents per hour. I knew there was more out there to see besides the world I was exposed to. I had the desire to see what was out there. I worked very hard, so why not take this trip?

On the train ride, I was so tired, but my babies were full of energy. Imagine me trying to rest while holding my energetic son on my lap and keeping an eye on a three and a half year old. A guy a little bit older than me was sitting across from me. He played with my kids and offered to watch my son so I could take a nap. I was so trusting, and I let him. Then, there was an older woman sitting next to me. She could pass as my mother. She also offered to watch my daughter while I nap. I was so trusting with strangers back then.

When I woke up, the kids were full of excitement. Those strangers kept them occupied and entertained. They called the older woman grandma during the rest of the ride. Once my son realized I was awake, he came and sat on my lap. The train stopped suddenly, and he hit his face on the seat in front of us. His nose began to bleed. I, of course, panicked. The sudden stop occurred because the train had broken down in New York City. While the staff made accommodations for the passengers on the train, the strangers came over to assist me with my son's bloody nose. I had a young man and an older woman walking with me as if we all knew each other for years.

Amtrak booked hotel rooms for all of the passengers and gave us cash. The older woman instructed them to book us in the same room. When we got to the hotel, the room was big and nice. She helped me bathe my babies and put white T-shirts on them. After a good night's rest, we went shopping the next day, ate delicious food, walked through the NYC crowd, and took pictures. While we enjoyed our day, she told me she lived in Atlanta. The kids continued to call her grandma as we enjoyed ourselves. The following day, we were ready to go back to the Amtrak train. My son had his own seat this time, and we got free food. I kept in contact with the guy and the older woman. But as years went by, we lost touch. However, I will never forget them as my assisting angels.

I have had the pleasure of being an assisting angel when things were much better for me. I was a manager at a shop. Finally, I had a reliable car and lived in a decent townhouse near my shop in the suburbs. I felt accomplished. One day, my oldest daughter, who was nine years old, got sick. I did not send her to school. I had to work, so I took her and my baby girl to my parents.

As I was driving, my intuition told me to take a different route. So, I went down a side street. I usually would take the highway road. There was a young Hispanic girl standing at a bus stop crying. Two huge Rottweilers were jumping and barking at her. I quickly opened my passenger door and told her to get in. The dogs continued to bark at her and followed her to the car. Thank God they didn't bite her.

I asked her where she was going. She said she was on her way to work at the mall. I gave her the phone to call her job to let them know she would be late. Another coincidence took place. Her job was on my way to my job. I dropped her off at the bus stop where she would originally get off.

That night, I had nightmares of the dogs jumping in the car and attacking my girls from the back. When I woke up, I had a vision of me being in my car. I could see a girl at a bus stop. She was crying because of two big Rottweilers. In my vision, I knew my girls were safe in the back seats. But, my subconscious mind had me reliving this moment with a different scenario. She may consider me as her earth angel. I quickly realized that I was directed to her for a reason. Nothing happens by coincidence.

Riding Angel

I was fortunate to always align my workplace near my children's schools. At the time, my baby girl was in first grade. We lived thirty minutes from her school and ten minutes from my job. I dropped her off at school in the mornings and headed to work afterward.

This particular day, I happened to notice a woman and her daughter walking to the same school. It was a very cold morning. I drove close to them, rolled down my window, introduced myself, and offered her a ride. She took me up on the offer and introduced herself as Mercedes. This became a routine of ours. I would text her on my way to school, meet them at their apartment parking lot, and bring them back from school.

By the way, it was hard teaching my child not to talk to strangers. Here I was, picking up a stranger. I just remembered how I felt when I had no transportation and had to walk in the cold weather. I felt bad for the child and mother.

Mercedes shared stories about her family and arranged marriage. I learned a lot about her Indian Culture and enjoyed her conversations and kindness. She even sent her husband to my shop for a haircut. A few times, she cooked Authentic Indian food and shared it with me. When her husband had to relocate back to India, we lost communication. I tried finding her on Facebook by searching for her name. It turned out there are a lot of Mercedess. Either way, I believe I was a blessing to her as she was to me. I will always remember them as they will remember us.

Loving Angel

I have experienced many loving angels. When I was a cashier, a Romanian couple and the wife's sister always came through my line on Tuesdays. Every Tuesday was Senior Citizen Day. They always gave me a lottery scratch-off ticket. I quickly got used to it and would not bring lunch on Tuesdays, because I expected to win a few bucks from a scratch-off and buy lunch at the store. They were so kind to me.

There was also a Greek gentleman who just loved my name. Growing up, I did not appreciate my name. It was uncommon and mispronounced. My name grew on me once he told me its meaning and origin. In Greek mythology, it means Goddess of the sea. I learned to appreciate my name from then on.

There was a lady who would grocery shop every Friday. She was a stay-at-home mom. She would open up her desserts and share them with me. One day, she told me her father talked me up. Come to find out, her father was the Greek man. Wow! It seemed like everyone I knew was connected to someone else that I came in contact with.

Once, when my car broke down, I had to walk one hour from home to work. I had no choice but to keep pushing through. It was a daily two-hour walk after standing eight hours on my feet. One day, I was walking home and saw an older Italian woman who shopped at the grocery store. She was working in her garden. She was so happy to see me and ran to me, put both hands on my face, kissed my cheek, and said, "Bella." I had never been kissed like that before. Maybe one cheek, but not two.

I was so young and did not understand the meaning of these people being drawn to me. I knew I was very friendly, pleasant, and polite, but this was a little overwhelming. As I began to pay attention and observe more, this became a norm for me throughout the years. I was connected to many people who were related, friends, or co-workers.

Networking of Angel

When I was working at one of the shops, an older man always came to get a haircut. He was so quiet. Honestly, for some reason, I was intimidated by him. He always requested me to serve him. A woman with two little boys also preferred me to be their stylist. One of her boys had blonde curly hair, and the other had brunette curly hair.

One day, the mother came in so excited. She explained that she was having Thanksgiving dinner, and her parents started discussing her father's haircut. Guess what! Her dad was the older man. Once again, it's another coincidence. I often ask why I keep meeting people who have a connection, but they do not even know I am the mutual connection.

Here is another similar experience. There was a young lawyer whose hair I had cut for years while working in Charlotte. He and his friends requested me as their preferred stylist. There was also an older man who always came in as a walk-in and requested me. But, I never got his first name. One day, he came in, and I remembered to ask him his name. I noticed he had the same last name as the young lawyer. Of course, I shared that with him, and it turned out he was the father of the lawyer.

I asked him if his son had referred me to him. His response was no. He was surprised that his son was getting haircuts by me as well. What were the odds? Father and son preferred the same stylist.

Sometimes, it was unbelievable. At one point in time, I even serviced two brothers. They were scheduled back to back. And once again, they requested me without me knowing they had the same stylist. One was a brunette, and the other one was redheaded. They did not favor one another. They greeted each other cordially, and later, one brother told me they were brothers but estranged.

Who's the Angel? I'm The Angel

The moment I am about to recount was quite fascinating. When I was working in Charlotte, a client came in. He had just arrived from Florida. He started talking about his visit to Florida and shared that he ran into someone who spoke about someone who knew me. Apparently, there was a client in Florida whose hair I cut who said he was serviced by yours truly. What a small world.

Here is another one. There was a flight attendant who I took care of. He came in for a cut and told me he was on a shift to California, and a passenger complimented him on his haircut. They complimented each other on their hair. He told her the shop's name and location. It turns out, the passenger told him that she went to the same shop as a walk-in. They both said to one another, "The girl with the purple hair in uptown." Yes, it was me. I took a risk wearing a purple wig and was remembered.

Serving Angels

When I lived in Rochester and worked at the shop, I became close with a few clients and their families. I became attached to them and developed a bond. They would invite my children and me to their homes for dinner and Thanksgiving dinners. I would make my rounds from my family and then to their places. I kept in contact with some of the families through social media.

Another client of mine was a Bishop. For some reason, he did not go to the barbershop in the city. He was drawn to come to me. At this time, I was less skilled with bald fades than I am now. I was decent. He chose me and trusted me. His wife was a Pastor, and they invited me into their home. I remember she told me she wanted to have a baby, and God was going to fulfill her wish. She did have her babies. She was reminding me about the power of manifesting, but I was not awakened to understand it. They were sent to me for a reason. They invited me to their church. I did visit, but they did not pressure me or discontinue our connection. It was something about me that they saw that I did not.

When I was living in Florida, they contacted me while they were on a trip to Florida. I went to see them at their vacation apartment. They did not have to contact me, but they did. They were so loving and caring. They both have passed; may they rest in peace. Nevertheless, I will always remember their kindness. I am connected with their son through social media to this present day.

A few years ago, I was at work, and a woman entered the shop with an envelope and asked for me. She handed me the envelope and stormed off. It was a Christmas card with money inside and a beautiful message. I still do not know who it was from. But, I kept the card.

Angels of Love

A few years ago, I was sitting in a hospital lounge room with a group of four, visiting someone. There was a young girl who walked by and looked directly at me. Then, she walked back by and came in with her parents. She was drawn to me and came directly to me as if she knew me. She was around the same age as my oldest granddaughter. I believe she was seven. She sat beside me, talking to me as if she already knew me, sharing her life story. She lived in Pennsylvania and was there visiting a sick family member. She was so adorable. She did not speak to anyone else in the room.

When it was time for her to leave, she excused herself for not properly introducing herself. She stood not too far from me and asked my name. I smiled at her and introduced myself back. I felt this warm feeling of joy. I now understand why she chose me out of everyone in the room. I needed the expression of love due to the circumstances of the visit to the hospital.

Another time, I was shopping at the grocery store. I had skipped lunch that day at work, because we were busy. I looked for something to eat in the hot foods section. The Deli's clerk was restocking the hot foods. She looked at me and smiled. I asked her a question about the food. She responded and then kissed me on the cheek. She was not too much older than me. But for some reason, she said I reminded her of her daughter.

Maybe she was a young mother like I am. This was yet another surprise. I had never seen this woman in my life. I was just hungry and wanted to grab some food before heading to my acting class. I was not looking for anything more than that. I did post that experience on my Facebook feed that day. It was different for me. I have experienced many more moments similar to these last two moments.

During the holidays, my customers would bring me gifts for my kids. I was so blessed to see the front-end runners direct them to a slower checkout lane, but they insisted on waiting for me to cash them out. My line was long, and they did not mind waiting for me. I was one of the top-best cashiers. I had my troubles, but I never brought them to work. I smiled no matter what

I was experiencing. I innately knew how to compartmentalize.

Understanding of Angels

I still do not have the answers to how all these people were drawn to me. I share this because it has been a part of my journey in life. I did not know why then, but now I have a better understanding as I continue to observe. I have always been drawn to great people. I have had and still have many earth angels. They have blessed me, especially during the Covid-19 pandemic. Even when I lost my business in 2020, many of my clients sent me blessings. I cried because I could not believe how much they cared about me and my family. I had zero income, and these angels gifted me.

As I reflect on these moments of my life, I begin to comprehend how each of us plays a role in another's life–in one way or another. Even if it's just a simple hello, thank you, smile, and so forth; it is healing. I realized every connection, rejection, and obstacle that occurred was for a purpose.

I overcame all of my trials and kept getting back on my horse. I became wiser and stronger with each experience. They were all lessons to learn from the school of life. I was given tools and learned to apply them when in need. I am sharing my experience with others so we can all elevate together. This is one of the many gifts from the one and only divine Creator!

Ephesians 1:11 (Spiritual Blessings)

"In whom also we have obtained an inheritance, being
predestinated according to the purpose of him who worketh
all things after the counsel of his own will:"

Day 

Releasing

Finally, winter was over; the snow was melting, the weather was getting warmer, the smell of Spring was in the air, and it was time to put away the winter boots, hats, scarves, heavy coats, and sweaters. Perfect timing. I was getting tired of the clutter in my closet. However, during this time, I procrastinated with everyday tasks. But finally, I decided, "Today is the day to be disciplined and get it done."

My walk-in closet was spacious enough to fit a twin-size bed and two dressers. So, there was a lot of work ahead of me. My intentions were to fill the boxes with everything that no longer fit me or did not serve me any purpose. Most of my clothes were pretty dresses, sexy tops, and jeans. I would sell some to consignment shops and donate the rest to Goodwill.

I've always had a hard time letting go of material things since I barely had clothes when I was younger. Just to let you know, I did understand the root of the reason for this. I had such a tough time letting go of everything I invested in financially. I recognized it then. It was a problem. I was becoming materialistic. Thankfully, I slowly learned to detach myself from material things over the years.

It was ten in the morning, and I was ready. I walked into my closet, and to the left and the right were stacks of laundry baskets full of clothes and clothes hanging on wooden hangers. I opened the window to smell the fresh air. I began removing the baskets from the closet to sort through them.

I stepped on something and heard, "OUCH!" All the hairs on my body stood up: goosebumps, chills, all of the above. I thought to myself, "Am I hearing voices?" I continued to clear out my closet. Then, I heard that same voice say, "OOH, WEE. Finally, I am free."

Me: What in the world? (A bright light began to expand right before my eyes. It looked somewhat like a brain with a feminine body form.)

She spoke to me, "Oh yeah, you're probably trying to process all this—no need to be afraid. I'm just your Mind. Boy, you have so many clothes here. I was smothered there. I could barely breathe." She takes a deep breath and then exhales as if she were in a meditative mode.

My Mind: I was waiting for you to finally declutter to give me some peace of mind. (Laughing.) Oh, never mind. Loosen up, will you? You have been so uptight lately. Geesh.

I ran to my bathroom and washed my face to see if I was hallucinating. I looked in the mirror, and there she was behind me. I just kept splashing cold water on my face. I closed my eyes, shut them tight, and then opened them back up. I slapped my face, looked in the mirror, and told myself, "You are seeing and hearing things. Wake up. I will definitely go to bed early to get my eight hours of sleep, for real."

My Mind: Ha. I know you see me, because for the first time I can see me. MMMMM… Not too shabby. I look pretty good. (With admiration, she looks at the mirror's reflection and places her hands on her waist.)

I saw a green light, and then it flashed to a red form coming out, as it came out of my reflection in the mirror.

Me: Oh shit, shit. I'm really losing it. What is going on here? (I backed away from my sink as the form floated over me and then stood next to me with an introduction.)

My Heart: Hey, I'm your Heart. Relax. Everything is all good in the hood.

I'm here to help you out with… Let's just call thissss… an intervention!!!

Me: An intervention? For who? Me? But why? I don't have any vice that I'm addicted to. (I looked over and saw MY MIND playing with my clothes.)

My Mind: Technically, you do! (Holding up one of my cocktail dresses.) See this? When was the last time you wore this? (She picks up a dress, holding it with both hands, and looks at me.) Look at this. It still has the tag on it. See, this isn't even your size. (She places the dress on me.) It's way too big for you. Why is it still here taking up space? Not addicted, you say? Mmhmm… (My Mind kept going through my closet.)

Me: In my defense, it was on sale, and I bought it a few years ago just in case I would go somewhere. That way, I don't have to go shopping at the last minute. All I have to do is go into my closet.

My Heart: Well, you don't want to go anywhere. So, why keep it, especially if it doesn't fit you?

My Mind: Look at all these wigs. Do you need these many for one person? (I noticed my mind putting on a wig, looking in the mirror, and blowing kisses to herself.) Ooh, look at me.

Me: You've got to be kidding me. Is this really happening? (I pinched myself.) Ouch! Aww, man. I really am looking at My MIND. (I stared at my mind.) You really have a sense of humor.

My Mind: Where did you think your sarcasm comes from? Yes, yours truly. (Looking at the mirror, still admiring herself in my clothes and one the purple wigs.)

My Heart: (Smiles) And, I get to experience all the good feelings. Now, let's get to decluttering and clearing up a lot of space.

Me: Ok, I know, I know! That's why I was cleaning my closet.

My Mind: You don't understand you have been blocking us.

Me: Blocking ya'll?

My Heart: We are a trinity. All of us together.

My Mind: I am the place where your thoughts occur. I can create mental movies for you. Your imagination is based on your thoughts. Thoughts are vibrations. He picks up the signal that attaches whatever emotional feeling you're having with that thought.

Me: Wait. You said he?

My Heart: Yes, she did. I am masculine energy, and Mind is feminine energy, like the Sun is masculine and the Moon feminine. At least, that's my understanding.

My Heart: I am your feelings. I help produce what you want into reality. Feeling is the secret ingredient.

Both: We are supposed to be coherent and harmonious as one.

Me: I am so confused right now. Please explain to me what you are talking about.

My Heart: (Speaking to Mind.) Should I explain, or do you want to?

My Mind: You can explain.

I'm looking at both of them, like, please tell me what is going on.

My Heart: Alrighty, so when Mind and I work together harmoniously, we become oneness. Your subconscious mind lives inside me.

My Mind: Your consciousness lives inside me. We become one mind when you are coherent. We are connected directly to God. Some may use other terms such as universe, source etc.

My Heart: I know you heard ASK, AND YOU SHALL RECEIVE. They also say to be careful what you ask for. Once you place your order out into the universe, there aren't any cancellations. So, be careful what you wish for. You are aware that we are energy. We have an innate intelligence. If you think of a negative or positive thought and have a feeling about it, then it's on its way. I receive a vibrational signal transmitted to the universe, and you receive what you manifested. I only know how to communicate with you inside through feelings. It's all similar to the way the internet works. You connect to wifi, and there is a hub. The signal is sent to the dish in space, and then you have access to the internet.

My Mind: You have heard a mind is a terrible thing to waste. I never really cared for that statement anyway. When you fall asleep, we marry and go to work for you. Whatever thoughts you think of before falling asleep, if you have a feeling, it is conceived and sent to the universe, and your manifestations become a reality. Does that make sense to you?

Me: Uhmm, not really. I am slightly confused and still wondering when you are going to take off that wig.

My Heart: (Giggles) Ok, we are like a genie for you. Whatever you imagine, we will bring it to fruition for you. You need to declutter all your negative thoughts in your MIND so we can operate from only positive thoughts. Then, we can begin to create a better outer world for you. How you keep all these clothes is how you have been keeping old thoughts from your old program of thinking. You are blocking us from experiencing an abundant life full of joy. The mind can conceive when you believe anything can be achieved. We all work together. We have to be aligned.

My Mind: I send the signals to every cell, organ, and muscle. For example, I signal your legs to keep walking even when you don't feel like walking. Your legs are yours to serve you. You really do not know how much power you have and how we are all here to serve you. You have your own team just for you and only you. But girl, you have me on overload. I am operating from your old habitual behavior. You are my master. I serve you. It's a battle. Your ego is inside me and wants to take over. Your ego only knows to protect you and what feels safe and familiar.

My Heart: I absorbed everything since you entered this world like a hard drive in a computer. You can unlearn and delete the old program. Reset and start with a better program. You are the only one who has the power to do it. You can choose which thoughts just by being mindful. If you have negative thoughts, pay attention to them. Then, quickly switch to a positive thought. Your inner thoughts reflect your outer world. We can be aligned directly with the source. That is how it was intended to be.

Me: Ok, so you both are telling me that I need to declutter my closet because it is a reflection of my inner thoughts in my mind. When I clear this space, my mind has room, and I have better control of my mind to think clearly. I then can sleep better; my mind is at ease so that both of you will reunite. Then, I use my imagination and get my wish fulfilled.

My Mind: Yes, see, it's simple—imagination and feeling it. The ninety percent of your true being is already living your wish fulfillment. It is waiting on the ten percent of you to be there.

My Heart and My Mind looked at each other and high-fived one another. They both said, "Here's to becoming extraordinary!"

There I was, staring at myself in my mirror, looking at my reflection, and wondering how I became the person I was in this present moment. I understood that my EGO was my personality due to my life experiences. It was my shadow side. But still, a part of me I had to embrace. However, I was not my body nor my mind. I could take control of my life story by being in the present moment and understanding who I truly was. I could command my mind and change my thoughts if I did not like how I was feeling.

My heart is the place where I express my love to other living beings. It is also where my frequency levels are high or low. Depending on how I allow myself to feel. My heart is the place where I connect directly to God. My mind absorbed a lot of my outer world. My mind is my consciousness, and my heart is my subconscious. When I align them together, I can accomplish so much more. My mind creates the visual, and with my feelings coming from the heart space, completes the process of bringing it into reality. It is a daily effort to practice this. I focus on raising my frequency with simple appreciations throughout my day.

My Ego Shaped the Old Me

Based on my childhood, my parents did the best that they could. I shared a room with my oldest sister. She slept on a full-size bed, and I slept on a used cot from a thrift store. Our closet was so empty. Two dresses were hanging on the hanger. My father bought us one new outfit for the first day of school and a few skirts and tops from the Salvation Army. We had at least seven outfits. They made sure we were always clean. My mom always did laundry on Saturdays.

The other kids would always pick at my wardrobe. My Salvation Army shoes were so worn out that a hole would be in the soles within a month of me wearing them. I could feel the ground when I walked. I dragged my feet so no one would notice them. I recall when I was in the eighth grade, one of my classmates would make fun of me. But one day, she told me I had a nice body, and all I needed was nice clothes.

My first job, I bought new clothes. I eventually realized I had a vice. As I looked in my closet and saw that I had bought the same dress/shirt twice at different times because it was on sale and I liked it. I would buy every color if I liked a dress, shirt, pants, skirt, and footwear. My daughters would say my closet looked like a store in the mall. I even had clothes with tags. I am grateful that I became self-aware and stopped the impulsive shopping.

I shopped at TJMax, Burlington, and Marshalls and bought my children marked-down name brands in every color of shoes and hats to match their outfits, only because I did not want them to be teased as I was. I wanted my children to have everything I didn't have. I would overspend on Christmas gifts as well, buying unnecessary items. When I realized I had an addiction to shopping, I told my daughter, when she was ten, not to let me buy anything at the store. After telling her to stop me from shopping, we went window shopping. As soon as we walked into the store, I saw a pretty pink hat with a matching purse. When I went to pay for an item, my poor daughter stopped me. I managed to convince her not this time, but the next time. I was obsessed with shopping.

Ruling My Ego

After cleaning out my closet and donating many things to charity, I saw more space and felt better. I did not realize that my inside thoughts and feelings expressed my outer world. I told myself that whenever I bought something new, I would donate what I was no longer wearing or using. I realize how much of our adult identities stem from our childhood experiences. I cut back on shopping to only when we needed it. I also became self-aware of my thoughts, feelings, and behavior. I was now an observer.

When something triggered a memory, I quickly switched it to a scene with a production team on set or paid attention to how it made me feel and then switched to a happy thought, or I would say I choose love, and the negative thought would go away. It has still been a work in progress, because the EGO still battles to take control. However, I feel better knowing that I have the power to choose better thoughts. I felt good about my accomplishments. I began to pay attention to my thoughts and feelings, being self-aware of everything in my world.

I recently did an exercise I had learned. I asked myself what my next thought was going to be, and I did not have a thought at all. I quieted my mind to get in touch with my heart. I imagined an invisible chord going straight out into the universe and plugging directly into God. I surrendered and let go of hanging on to attachments from old ways of believing my repeated past experiences. My mind was so used to believing old habitual behaviors. I avoided overanalyzing and overthinking and started focusing my attention inward, focusing within myself, paying attention to how I was feeling and my breathing.

I stopped thinking about my past and began to imagine my future in the present as if I was already living it. I told my youngest son to treat our town-home like it is our mansion. He is an artist and can be messy. This was my way of motivating him to clean up and appreciate what he has in the present moment. I shared the details of my dream house with a nice backyard with him so he would have a mental picture in his mind. However, he suggested we get a mansion with a butler. He has his own vision. So, now my dream house has turned into a mansion. It did not happen overnight for me to finally realize I was hurting myself with my thoughts and fears; holding on to the old way of being was keeping me dormant.

Thoughts are energy and hold the power to create our outer world. I learned to observe my thoughts and feelings by taking a moment to stare at a hibiscus flower on my patio. I would just focus on the flower, as if I were examining the flower. As I touched each pedal, I found my mind was silenced. I admired its beauty and the aroma scent. I was not thinking about yesterday or the next day. I was lost in the hibiscus flower's beauty and being present in the moment. I was feeling at ease and grateful.

Apparently, no one knows where thoughts come from, and every person has thousands of thoughts running every minute. I have learned that thoughts are a form of energy. The more you pay attention to a fear of thought, the more energy it receives and expands. I now know that when a negative thought pops into my mind, with one simple change, I choose a positive outcome, and I am capable of creating better mental movies. I am the executive producer, director, and writer of the story.

I practice setting my intention on a daily basis with awareness of how I am feeling. We are all innate, powerful beings. We simply do not know how to operate our minds to the full capacity. We did not come to this world with a manual. Mankind created them along the way. Although animals did not come here with a manual as well, they, on the other hand, live through their natural intelligence.

When a bird is expecting her offspring, she naturally knows. She does not need a pregnancy test. Birds know how to weave a sturdy nest for their eggs without instructions from an institute. Animals are aligned directly to The Divine. We tend to ignore our natural instinct. Conformity has been passed down from generation to generation. I pray for guidance, unblocking of any blockages, understanding of life, and to observe and watch the process. So, I can only share based on my experiences.

At times, when I am in a meditative state thinking, I would think of someone, and they would either call or text. I may also see them in person. I have had conversations about this topic with others, and they seem to resonate. We are indeed all connected. I never understood why everyone I came in contact with was connected to someone from my past or present. Now, with social media, you can see so many of us have mutual connections all over the world.

I remember once while working at the grocery store as a cashier, I checked out a customer and recognized her scent, then her face. She was my kindergarten teacher. I was living at least thirty minutes from the school I attended in 1980. I, of course, was surprised she recognized me, and she said I still had the same face. I was in my early twenties.

Around this same time, my car broke down. I had some spare change. Someone suggested the nearest bus stop was a thirty-minute walk, better than the full one-hour walk in the heat. As I got on the bus, I saw an old classmate sitting in the front seat. She and I were in kindergarten and eighth grade together. At that moment, I had a flashback. I had seen her in my dream the night before. I was so naive I said it to her. She looked at me like I was crazy. I was embarrassed and understood she had not seen me in over a decade. Why would I see her in my dream? Back then, I didn't understand that we all have experienced this, but only a few know how to tap into it. I have yet to master it myself. I have known others who have shared their dreams, and they came true.

I experienced it once again at another time. I was at this new spot in uptown Charlotte. I was hanging out with an acquaintance and her friends at Merchant and Trade uptown. A few years later, I was on my way to the shop and saw one of my acquaintance's friends walking toward me. At that moment, I had a flashback of my dream the night before. I greeted them, but this time, I stopped myself from telling them I saw them in my dream the night before, and I continued walking to work.

While working in uptown, I was attracted to a CPA who worked at the bank. We hung out a few times. Then, with time, it faded away. One morning, as I walked to the shop, I was reminiscing about him, and within two seconds, he was crossing the street towards my side. He was fifty feet from me. Some may call it a coincidence, but this happened to me a lot. I believe we all may have experienced it, though sometimes we wake up and can not remember our dreams.

I was triggered to remember when I saw the two people early in my day on my way to work. Both were different times and different states, but similar experiences. We are too busy caught up in this world with everyday life and tend to miss a lot.

As I am writing this, I remember graduating from Beauty College. I moved from one place to another. I could not find my black hard rubber comb. I needed it to take the State Practical Exam. One night, I fell asleep thinking about my lost comb. In my dream, I saw my comb full of blood in the blue case with the other hair supplies. Our Cosmetologist instructor had us use red nail polish to put our initials on our belongings. It made sense why I saw red blood in my dream. I woke up and went to the place I saw in my dreams, and there was my comb with my initials in red. Again, I did not understand all of this and am still learning as I go. But, I have experienced so much that I know there is more to us than we know.

I learned to switch my thoughts as if I were switching the channels on a T.V. remote. I am a spiritual being inside a human body, experiencing life as an expression of God. God is one power, and we are a part of him. You would think we should have had all of our innate gifts mastered. Life would be a simple breeze in paradise. Unfortunately, it is not. I stopped questioning and began to understand more as I continued my journey.

I came across more beings who had a better understanding than I did. I trust the process of life and work on doing my part in it. I still do not know the significance of most of my experiences, other than I had to go through it all to be in the place that I am today. However, I have found peace within myself.

"A time to search and a time to give up, a time to keep and a time to throw away,"

Day 5

Forgiveness

Feeling hopeless and alone, I closed my eyes and had a long conversation with the Divine, The Creator. I asked him why, "Why do I get hurt so much by close connections full of betrayals and deception? I am skeptical when it comes to trusting others." He responded, "Well, my Love, this is what your soul signed up for before entering the portal through your mother's womb to come to the Earth. Your soul signed several contracts with other souls before you went into a deep sleep. You were supposed to wake up once you completed several lessons and passed the tests. Then, you would remember your true mission on Earth. You will see signs reminding you that you're being guided on the right path. You only need to trust yourself, knowing you will be able to discern better."

Me: Ok. But, why did I agree to sign contracts to get hurt repeatedly? And, most of these people who hurt me never have remorse or apologized. That makes no sense to me."

Divine: Well, you did, and it's part of your growth process. And every time you prayed for strength, I sent you more challenging situations so you could become stronger.

Me: What? Why would you…? I mean, I thought praying for help was supposed to help me, not put me in a desperate state of being.

Divine: Well, I gave you what you asked for. Remember that saying holds a lot of power. ("Be careful what you ask for.") To gain strength, you have to experience hardships. How else do you suppose you would be who you are becoming? You can call it Earth School. With each lesson learned from an experience, you level up. Unfortunately, there were some you did not grasp.

So, I had to throw you another one until you got the lesson. Sometimes, I had to interfere to test you to see if you learned from past experiences.

Me: Yeah, that part. I realized that much. From now on, I am paying attention to what I say or ask. I will be very specific about what I ask you for. I have a long list of wants and needs.

Divine: See, you are getting the hang of it. I knew you would. You must begin forgiving yourself first, just like I forgave you. You lost hope in me for some time, but I knew you would come around. I was glad you found your way back to me. I sent you guidance and protection along the way. I gave you the time you needed to find the space in your heart. Now, here you are, and I am here with you.

Me: Why do I have to forgive myself and others? I am nothing like you. I am human, have feelings and a memory like an elephant. It's hard to forget the pain. It is much like a sharp knife going through your back and right through your heart.

Divine: Now, that is where you are so wrong. You are like me. I created you in my image. It's time to forgive yourself and everyone who has caused you pain and grief—no apologies needed. You can forgive and not have them in your world. Send them love and blessings. Most of them are still operating from their EGO low vibrations. Otherwise, they would have recognized their behaviors and held themselves accountable for their actions. You, on the other hand, have to let go of all the pain and any memory attached to it. Resentment only blocks so many blessings from being received. It hurts you more than the pain they caused. It grows inside you like fungus. Do not allow yourself to be clogged up. Release the hurt and unclog what is not meant to reside in your heart space. You were created to love. You are one with me and one with your brothers and sisters. Everything I created is one with me. Most of them may still be asleep, but you are awakening slowly but surely. It is now time for forgiveness so you can begin operating only from love to all living beings. Your true essence is love. For I am love, and you are my creation. Love is the key to becoming who you were meant to be. You're becoming extraordinary!"

Me: Are you serious? No apologies needed?

Divine: I Am!

I Lost It All, To Gain It All

It all began to unfold for me during COVID-19 pandemic. The world was locked down, and I lost my primary source of income. I have always been the provider for my family. I lost 95% of my income. I was so afraid my children and I were going to be homeless. When I drove uptown, I saw many tents outside for the homeless. My mind took me there, fearing it would be my children and me. All I knew was to provide for myself and my family. I panicked and geared to survival mode.

I started binging on Netflix, eating the worst foods, drinking wine, and watching the news while it promoted fear. I had stocked up on canned goods, foods, and toilet tissue. I sequestered myself and became a hermit. I panicked and was afraid of being alone with my children and granddaughter.

Soon, I began to pray for a better understanding of life besides what I already knew by faith and experience. Deep down, I knew there was more than the books I learned from. I had my curiosity about my connection to the Earth, the universe, and everything around me. I began comparing my body to the Earth and the universe. The water percentage in a human being averages approximately 75 percent, and the water percentage of the Earth is 71 percent. The top four atoms in the human body are hydrogen, oxygen, carbon, and nitrogen, and they are also the most important elements of the Earth that allow life to exist.

I asked God for clarity on this information, and I received it—however, it was not the way I expected. I was receptive, and it began to make sense to me. I had read self-help books, but I was not receptive. They became self-shelf books after sitting on my shelves for a while. I learned it only makes a difference in your life if you understand and apply what information you learned and practice the principles in your daily routine. I realized that as I closed out each cycle in my life, things almost seemed so coincidental, and how things unfolded so rapidly.

During the Spring of 2020, it was a chaotic time for everyone. The first pandemic in my lifetime. I came across several podcasts from positive influencers. I became receptive and eager to learn and understand the meaning of my being—the causations of all that I had endured. I was on autopilot for a long time in survival mode. Sometimes, I could not remember how I got from point A to point B. I signed up for one-time free Zoom classes, meetings, and webinars every Thursday during the pandemic for inspiration as an aspiring actor. Something inside of me was pushing me to prepare myself. A part of me would not let it go. These Zoom meetings and classes were my highlights of the week. My outer world was in shambles, but deep down inside me, I had the hope that things would get better one day. I began to apply myself to prepare for the greatness that would soon come my way.

This was a process as I learned to de-stress and manage self-mastery. I found myself looking for the inner switch to turn my light back on. I had so many blockages that I had to go deep within to search for the breaker circuit inside me to turn my light on. It was as if I was in a labyrinth. Once I found the breaker box, I replaced all the old fuse and made sure all circuits were up and running properly to maintain my light from within me. I began to feel different, such as at peace and calmness. I was trusting the process of life.

Everyone was adapting to the new norm that was taking place during the COVID-19 pandemic. I was able to return to work in June. Everyone did not return to work or live the everyday life we were accustomed to. It was extremely slow and depressing at work. I had a few brave clients who came to get serviced. I was averaging five to ten clients a week. It was still below minimum wage. Anyone close to me knew I was struggling. I had to accept my new norm, the world's new norm. This statement, "Be grateful for what you have," was in my thoughts heavily. This was a major wake-up call for me. My life was like ashes on the floor.

It was late October, and unforeseen events took place. My left shoulder began to hurt, and I was not thinking clearly. I was in such an emotional state of mind. My shoulder was hurting so bad that I placed an ice pack directly on my skin. Immediately, a red circular shape was developed. I could not move my left arm, and my lips felt numb. I went to the emergency room, and my blood pressure was 160/120. I was diagnosed with frozen shoulder/tendinitis, and the X-rays showed calcium deposits.

My doctor referred me to physical therapy. He did not focus on my blood pressure. Normally, I would have dealt with my shoulder pain, but God had other plans for me. It was like a ripple effect. I had a client scheduled on this day and was determined to serve him with the pain. I needed to provide for my children. I had to go to work at all costs, and so I did.

The pain continued, so I went to Urgent Care three days later. They were not accepting any more patients. I was in despair, because I was not feeling well and knew something was wrong with me. The doctor came outside, took me, and had me sign in. She examined me and told me I was healthy enough and to stop stressing. She quoted some scriptures from the Bible and told me, "Look in the front mirror of your vehicle. There is a reason for the rearview mirror being so small. It is a reminder to leave the past behind you and continue to look forward."

I was diagnosed with high blood pressure and prescribed Amlodipine. As I shared my new diagnosis, it seemed like everyone was on the same medications. I was never a person who depended on medication. When I had my last C-section, I asked the nurse to stop giving me Percocet. They thought I was crazy. I opted out of oxycodone as well.

I was unhappy being diagnosed with a condition and placed on daily meditations. I voluntarily stopped attending my therapy session, because I kept accumulating more medical bills and financial stress. Eventually, my shoulder healed on its own.

However, here I was with a prescription, a mandatory daily medication. I was so disappointed in myself for allowing this to take place. I could not retrieve how because I had been on autopilot for the majority of my lifetime. I asked myself how I let it get this far. I knew I had to make a major shift in my life, in my world, for myself and my children. I had to lead by example.

After a week of being in my new condition, I was booked for a music video shoot that Saturday. I was not going to miss out on another opportunity due to fear. I played the older mom and, at the last minute, the younger version of the mom. Unfortunately, the actress for the younger mom tested positive for COVID-19. It was a long day in pain, but I pushed through. My arm was still hurting, and I could not move it as much.

During one scene, I had to cry. The director told me to relate my scene to my daughters when they were teens. I told her my girls were good girls and did not experience drama with them. However, the tears came so naturally because I was going through the pain in my world. I cried a river of tears. It was an amazing opportunity.

I began to walk for one hour daily. I cut back on all unhealthy foods and drinking and managed my thoughts. By February 2021, I had lost a good amount of weight and was training in a commercial class. I was invested in myself and did not worry about not bringing full-time income. I took a leap of faith. It was a reminder that I was on the right path.

My first supporting role in a faith-based feature film, Redeemed, was released on BET Plus. I had the opportunity to play opposite Keshia Knight Pulliam and TC Stallings. It was a great experience. I learned a lot and was beyond grateful.

I continued my training in acting. I found it to be therapeutic for everything. I kept the positive podcasts in mind that aligned with my craft. I understood my life experiences were not by accident. Everything began to unfold with a domino effect in my favor.

Nine months prior, Fatal Attraction was released on TVOne. I played the role of the mother of the victim. I could not share this with anyone until it was released. We filmed at the beginning of March 2020 before the shutdown. The unfortunate crime took place in my hometown, Rochester, New York. Most of my friends back home knew the family of the victim. It is a small world, after all. I was full of joy. Watching my children watch their mom on television was an exciting moment.

I always felt that I was raising my children as a single mother, all alone. But now I am aware that behind the scenes, I always had my spirit guides and angels helping me through it all. My higher self would not allow me to remain complacent no matter how many times I got knocked down hard.

As you know, I had gotten to the hardest part of my life. I allowed it to affect my emotional and physical health. However, as I watched my children's eyes light up as they watched me on the tube, I reminded myself I had to get up, even if it was in slow motion, as long as I got up and kept pushing forward. Just like a toddler when they realize they can walk after taking a few steps. They begin with standing and feeling comfortable with being able to stand without falling. Then, they take that first step and run.

The spiritual being is much more powerful than the dormant human being. I activated the power within myself. I had blocked myself from being who I was truly meant to be. Each course was something to learn from, apply to my everyday life, and pass it along to those who would be receptive.

As I raised three children, I learned each lesson and gained new tools. I am still raising my youngest and still learning. I share each lesson with my children so they can apply them in their lives. They watched me struggle and saw that I was resourceful. Above all, they watched me love unconditionally. Deep down, I knew they chose my soul as their mother here on Earth in this lifetime to guide them through their journey. I know my purpose in their life is to lead them righteously. I desire each of us to awaken and live abundantly in peace, love, and light.

I Obeyed

I decided to make a drastic change in my life. I chose to forgive myself and everyone who had hurt me, even without an apology for my peace. I worked hard to unlearn an unhealthy lifestyle. I went from unhealthy eating to eating healthy, walked daily for one hour with my children on the greenway, began to connect more with nature, listened to Solfeggio's frequency, and joined inspirational Zoom meetings and classes. I avoided anything that was toxic to eat and anything toxic to my mind and soul.

Through my major transformation, I listened to new thought authors' audiobooks, connected with crystals, began to let go of the fear of not bringing in a steady income, worked on my personal development, and changed my behavior patterns. I learned to trust myself more. The most exciting part of this transformation was the hard work I put into my acting craft. Even though I did not have a steady income, I continued to invest in myself for a better outcome, and I found it fulfilling.

I changed my mindset from "Why is this happening to me?" to "This is happening for me." I avoid the news or negative conversations. I became self-aware of how the things of my outside world would make me feel. I realized I was an empath. I absorbed so much energy. I learned to release what was not benefiting my emotional and mental health. I was making purchases as if I had a steady income. And, I was being blessed by angels. I trusted the process of life. Slowly, I began to let go of fear, stimulation, and anxiety. I began to appreciate what I noticed in the present moment. I practiced keeping my energy present. I was reflecting inward.

Facing many adversities helped me face what I no longer wanted. I began to understand my true connection with my higher self. As I continue to evolve, I have to keep reminding myself what to bring along with me and what to dispose of. I had to work on letting go of old habits, traits, thoughts, and behaviors. I now had new endeavors paved out in my journey.

Those old beliefs that had once remained were because I continuously repeated them naturally. I focused on self-discipline—a little every day. Every day with the work, I improved inwardly, reflecting on my external world. I began to trust the process of life as we trust the Earth is traveling around the sun. That is the one topic no one questions: Is the Earth on track and so forth?

I continued to lose my Covid weight and the extra weight I had put on over the years. I went from size 16 to size 4. I did not realize I was stuck for almost a decade, because of resentment and feeling guilty. A low vibrational place that kept me complacent. I still was not pleased with being diagnosed and on medications. I asked my doctor if I could discontinue the medications. I researched natural healing properties. My doctor was on board, and my follow-up in December 2021 revealed that my numbers had lowered. I did the work, and my work was paying off. I felt accomplished. I now knew I had the will inside me to make a difference in my body. I had set intentions and achieved great results. I was committed and dedicated to bettering myself.

In February 2022, the shop's owner passed away, RIP, on my granddaughter's birthday. He was one of the best human beings I have ever met. His death was heartbreaking. I received the news after leaving my nine-year-old son's annual physical. He was sad as well and said he had lost his best friend. When I would come home from work, my son would always ask how the owner was doing. He cared deeply for him. He enjoyed sweeping for him on the days I would take him to work with me. The owner would pay him. My son was pleased to earn some cash.

After this time, I began to listen to a money mantra on YouTube. By the way, it worked for me. Any time I listen to this, I receive a financial blessing. I found peace during this time.

My doctor took me off one of the blood pressure medications. And finally, in July 2022, my doctor took me off my last blood pressure medications and monitored me for a month without them. In August 2022, I was officially off my medications.

Then, the time came for my youngest daughter to go to college. I had to cut the umbilical cord. She was homeschooled, and sending her into the world was a big deal. During this time, I was busy traveling to filmings back to back. I was so grateful for these opportunities that I failed to take care of my health again. I was not sleeping or eating as well. When traveling, you tend to eat what is easy to access. Nine out of ten, it's fast food. Unfortunately, it's not always the healthiest.

Labor Day of that year came, and I drove to Atlanta for an in-person call back for Stranger Things: The Experience. I had not had a good night's sleep due to anxiety. When I returned home, I received an audition invitation from a well known Casting Director. I was excited and panicked because my daughter was my audition partner and camera person. I relied on her for my auditions. I became codependent on her.

As the days passed, I improved my diet, but was not feeling better. I checked my blood pressure. It was high due to the stress. I still had my medications in the bottle. I took both of them. I was so disappointed in myself. I felt like I was going backward after all the hard work.

I called my doctor's office after hours. The nurse on call advised me to find someone to immediately drive me to the hospital. My nine-year-old son heard the call and began to cry. I did not have anyone to drive me. My older children were thirty minutes away. My son was at a wedding, and my daughter was at the grocery store. I calmed my son down and prayed for guidance to reach safe and sound, and we did. I was ten minutes away from the hospital, so I drove myself. I was conscious and felt fine, other than my blood pressure reading.

While waiting there for hours, I listened to lower blood pressure frequency on YouTube. When they checked, my blood pressure was back to normal. MY EKG results were normal. I was diagnosed with insomnia, and they determined my sodium and potassium levels were too low. The side effects of low sodium were seizures.

The low sodium was from me completely removing salt from my diet.

Due to me drinking too much water, my potassium levels were too low. I went overboard being healthy. I was advised to add salt and drink less water. I did and also read about fresh beets. I ate so many beets when I went for my follow-up that my creatine levels were high. Apparently, too many beets are not good for your health. Yet, it helps with your blood pressure.

I managed to convince my doctor to allow me to go naturally. I avoided social media, ate healthily, prayed, meditated, and listened to healing frequency with my crystals. I said my daily affirmations, spoke to my body out loud and did more research on the vagus nerve and blood vessels.

On October 31, 2022, my blood pressure, sodium, potassium, and kidney levels were back to normal. When I took charge of my mind, I made it happen. My doctor kept me on the sleeping medications until my sleeping patterns were back to normal. I fell asleep to healing frequencies and woke up feeling peaceful and rejuvenated.

The management of this chaotic world was the challenge. I expressed to my doctor all the research I had been doing. If a small white pill can send a signal to my brain to tell my blood vessels to relax, why couldn't I do that myself? She agreed but also said it was not that easy. Here I was causing myself to be diagnosed with a condition due to fear of losing my income during the pandemic and unnecessary circumstances.

Then, I had another health scare with my breasts. I had to have a biopsy. It was benign tissue. I am grateful that I am well. However, the new medical bills added to my financial stress. I had just finished paying for the doctor's bill from the emergency in 2020. I told myself this happened for a reason. I did not panic as I did in 2020. I just believed it would be taken care of. This was another nudge to wake me up. Something was happening in my body. I did not check my Facebook, Instagram, or emails for weeks.

For years, when I experienced miracles and shared them with my children, they would tell me that I needed to write a book. My entire life has been a testimony of faith. There was a time that I intended to, but it would be a fictional book. I had my journals, and being down for a couple of weeks pushed me to write my book with the guidance of my mentor. I was still feeling ill. However, I completed my assignments. I began to share more of my story on paper the old-school way.

I had completed my first draft within two weeks. I was waking up in the middle of the night with downloads and began to write them down. I felt good about it and proceeded, and here I am. I believe my body was going through something, getting rid of my old self. I was instructed to sit down, stay away from social media distractions, and share my story.

I removed all my veils and became vulnerable. I did my research on what is the root cause of high blood pressure. Sleeping is a must for the body to regulate itself. We heal ourselves while we sleep. When the body is stressed, the mind sends signals to the brain, and the body goes into survival mode. I proved I could do better with my diet. I added salt and some not-so-good things to my diet to bring balance. I gained a few pounds, but I am still on the healthy scale.

I will admit I have been eating less healthier than I was prior, but my body can tell the difference, so now I am practicing managing it better. I am taking the time to work on extreme self-discipline to do better with my mind and forcing my mind to relax, so I can sleep better and recharge while I sleep. Balancing was the key, as that is an everyday challenge for me. But with practice and self-awareness, I am on the right path, working on getting better every day in every way.

I continued researching how our mind works and the vagus nerve. When under stress, the blood vessels contract, and blood pressure elevates. I had clarity that negative thoughts could create resistance and thus cause stress on the body. Thoughts can become things good or bad. During my personal development, working on healing and self-regulation, I stopped worrying about not making enough money to pay bills. This was the first time I sat down and trusted the process with both feet. I still was not working full-time. Occasionally, I worked a small job here and there and made ends meet.

I began to use my time wisely and only listened to positive and inspirational podcasts. I surround myself with like-minded people. I embraced the awareness that I was an empath. I had been operating from a low-vibration place for the majority of my life. Now, I understand that I can control my thoughts by clearing out the negative energy, as we all do. I became more mindful of where I was placing my focused energy. I avoided watching or listening to anything that would disturb my peace. I thanked God, for providing shelter, food, and resources for me. I practiced meditating and was able to quiet my mind. I became self-aware of my feelings. I had to go deep within my roots.

During this pandemic, I had an awakening. I had to go after my dreams as an actress, no matter my financial circumstances. I surrendered to joy, learned to trust life's process, and understood that God lives within me and every living being. He is the one higher power. Some consider him to be Source, Divine, and other names. He created us in his own image.

I had broken the generational curse of scarcity and lack of mindset and began filling my cup, nurturing myself, loving myself unconditionally, and connecting directly to the source. I had a lot of deep-rooted work to do going inward. Just like an Oak tree that has been cut down, all that is left is the stump and deep roots underneath and sometimes slightly above the ground. No man can cut through those deep roots to eliminate 100 years of roots. I at least had less than half a century of roots. I had to go deep within to remove it permanently, start fresh with fresh soil, plant new seeds, and keep watering them. I began to transform into a better version of myself.

Battling with the thoughts in my mind and my EGO taking over my body, I had to get rid of my perception of what I was not, the unfocused energy of uncertainty I had about myself. It was the old version of me. I felt whole and complete when I paid attention to my thoughts and feelings and quickly changed to positive thinking, with good feelings supporting that thought.

I overcame so many challenges of adversity throughout my entire life. It was time to make a change for the better. I was paying attention to my surroundings and thanking God for all of their existence—the benefits I had from this understanding of living in the present moment. I began creating a mental picture as if it were a movie, visualizing my future and setting my intentions. I was operating from my shadow side for years with my innate ability.

I learned to resolve the issues within my shadow side. I was in hermit mode and did not realize it until my health shook me. I had gotten knocked down harder than ever. I stopped playing and chose to make a change. I realized I disliked the script I had lived in for so many years. I could choose to be better and stop praying for strength. I experienced pain, suffering, sadness, betrayal, anger, resentment, frustration, and so on. It was time to experience love, abundance, joy, happiness, success, prosperity, peace, and freedom.

I invested in myself, working on daily affirmations and self-motivation, self-love, and care inward and outward. I was receptive and ready for more knowledge for my next chapter. I was not only eating healing food, but I was also feeding my soul what it had been yearning for, for quite some time. My EGO was no longer in the driver's seat. I am in the driver's seat, feeling good about it all.

I have always practiced gratitude, but I have now begun a new habit in my household. My children participate with me. Something they can repeat with their families. We write down grateful notes and put them in an empty vase. My daughter was away in college, and she makes sure she still writes her grateful notes to bring them home and place them in the vase. On December 31, we all sit down, drink sparkling wine with snacks, and read them out loud. We laughed because my son could not read his handwriting. We get excited when goals are completed. Overall, it's a great experience to share with my loved ones on the last day of the year. We begin again on January 1 with an empty vase for the new year and fill it up with gratitude notes.

I Gained Freedom

The day that I forgave myself first and accepted myself, then forgave everyone else who hurt me, was the day I found freedom in my own body. However, it did not mean they were back in my life. I had to release the resentment in my heart caused by the pain. This is when I began to operate from my heart, where love resides. My new journey began to unfold for the better.

I kept my faith in God, though I was still not bringing in a steady income. I was still surviving and pursuing my passion for acting and self-discovery. I have booked leads, principal roles, and supporting roles and made great connections. My family and a few of my clients continued to bless me. I knew I had to continue and thank God and my higher self for everything. I stopped looking at my outer circumstances and began looking at my inner world. The one world I had been neglecting for years.

I am in a peaceful state of mind and a better space. I got knocked down only to rise like a phoenix from the ashes. I had two choices: keep living my life with conformity and familiarity or take a leap of faith in the unknown and intend for a better life here on Earth. I chose to be better to myself.

I continued doing the work. I went within my entire existence. I had to delete my old program of thinking and begin a new, better program. Taking this first step and training yourself to be disciplined takes a lot of work. It doesn't happen overnight, but doing the work within is a start. I just wanted to be directly aligned to the Source. I was well aware I wouldn't make it far without being connected to him directly, just like a floral plant. It remains alive longer when its stem is still connected to the source of its existence. Once it's clipped off, it can only last a few days in a watered vase. God is the one source. God is pure consciousness. God is infinite intelligence. He is omnipotent. Who would we all be without God? God created us all in his image.

We were blessed with the gift of imagination to co-create our dreams and desires. I am living proof of it. I have asked, and I have received, even in the obstacles I have had to endure. When I prayed for strength, I received obstacles and challenges to become stronger. I asked for guidance and a better understanding of life. I got knocked down and redirected to the right path. I have learned from so many lessons.

When I was that teenager who didn't like to go to school and wished for a blackout or told the teacher I wasn't feeling good just to avoid exams or class, it worked out for me. Back then, I was using an innate power within me, and it manifested. At that time, I wasn't aware that thoughts and feelings were so powerful. I am grateful that I released resentment and pain. I am now self-aware and feel blissful.

Matthew 6:14

"For if ye forgive men their trespasses, your heavenly
Father will also forgive you:"

Day 

Synchronicity

I found myself in the center of a majestic rainforest surrounded by beautiful tropical birds, breathtaking pristine waterfalls, and lagoons. The hibiscus trees were yellow, red, and orange, and there were unfamiliar bright red-orange floral bushes around me. I ate fresh fruits from the trees' vines and drank fresh water from the river. In the river were white, pink, and red lotuses. The scent in the air was enticing.

As I listened to the sound of the crickets singing and birds chirping, I noticed that I was naked and barefooted. I found myself to be in solitude, blissful with my surroundings. Suddenly, I felt this hot breeze, and the leaves on the trees were blowing in the air. The bright sun was beaming on my face. A soft feminine voice says, "I see you are getting familiar with the rainforest."

I looked around to see where this voice came from and saw a golden light and a feminine form. The form was not human, but wore a purple floral crown with long dark green dreaded head adornment. It stretched down like a bridal wedding dress' train. Her hair was fanned out on the ground in a perfect form. It surrounded the entire area where I was standing. Her contour was voluptuous, her skin was a blend of red and brown, and she had sandy brown eyes, mesmerizing, something out of this world.

She says, "I know you are confused. I can feel your confusion. I am Mother Gaia. Some know me as Mother Earth." I was taken by her beauty and soothing voice.

Me: How did I end up here? I was walking the Greenway and found myself here. I couldn't find my way back to my car.

Mother Gaia: My dear, you have unlocked several portals, and now you can come and go as you please.

Me: With all due respect. I love it here, but I can't live here forever. I have to get back to my family. If I can come and go as I please, why haven't I been able to go back to the Greenway?

Mother Gaia: You asked for understanding, and I am here to show you better than telling you.

Me: What is it that you want me to see?

Mother Gaia strolls through the pastures, coming to a halt before an immense screen resembling a clear crystal ball strategically placed at the core of the rainforest. With a sweep of her hand, she gestures to the left, engaging with the expansive display. "Is this even real?" I thought to myself.

Mother Gaia: See here. (She pointed at the enormous screen. It was the apartment I lived in for five years.)

Me: Why are you showing me my old apartment?

Then, she swiped again at another location where I lived.

Mother Gaia: I want you to see that you were always at the right place at the right time every time. The number of that apartment you lived in was 1111. You didn't understand the meaning of those numbers back then, but now you have a better understanding. You experienced so many struggles and learned many lessons. Your innate wisdom helped you to continue pushing through.

Me: Yes, I am still learning as I go.

Mother Gaia: Yes, I know. It took you a while to connect with me. And, we are finally happy that you have. I just wanted to let you know nothing was by coincidence. You are here in this present moment for a reason, and deep down, you know your purpose. I am very proud of you. I always have been. Come this way. You have been here for six days now. You were having so much fun you did not even notice.

Me: Six days? Oh no, my kids. They must be worried. I need to get back. How can I get back?

Mother Gaia: Relax, my child. Your kids are fine. That's one thing I can do that they will not even realize it's been six days, just like you did not notice. I can manipulate time, and you can too. You will be back just in time to cook supper.

Me: Ok, great. I don't want to seem ungrateful. I enjoyed my time here. It was magical and definitely memorable, so peaceful listening to the natural sounds of nature. But, I really have to get back.

Mother Gaia: I know you did. And, so many take precious moments in life for granted. Come and step on this boulder right here. It will take you back to the Greenway. Remember to love and keep a pure heart. You're becoming extraordinary!

Me: Thank you, Mother Gaia.

Then she vanished into the air. I stepped on the third boulder in my path and was back on the Greenway's trail. What an extravagant experience that was. No one would believe me even if I told them. I made it back to my car.

My life began to change for the better when I lived in the 1111 apartment. At that time, I was not aware of it. I was more focused on the glass being half empty. It was August 2019, right before the pandemic. Something inside me told me to start looking for a house to lease and put my house on the market. My realtor showed me several locations for a few months until I found the right one. I signed the lease the day before Thanksgiving.

A few years prior, my daughters helped me lay out laminate flooring on the lower level of the house. I started pulling out the carpet with them, but my knees could not handle it. My girls took over and ripped the rest of the carpet and padding. They placed each plank on the lower level. My daughters were committed and determined. They moved the heavy furniture and worked late nights. I finished helping with the final touches. They did a good job for their first time. The labor was tough, but they were resilient.

I remember when the employee at Lowe's thought I was crazy when I placed my supply order. He laughed at me. My previous maintenance man also laughed at us. I raised amazing daughters. I put my house on the market after the New Year. Within no time, I had several offers. I chose the investor's cash offer. The process began with the due diligence fees paperwork, etc.

In March 2020, the world was on shutdown. The investor pulled out and wanted to negotiate for less than he originally offered. I told my realtor, no way and to pull the house off the market. I trusted in God. He would guide me.

A couple of months went by slowly, and the country removed some restrictions. We put the house back on the market. I got several offers. The one I chose mailed me the due diligence check with her returning address, Apt# 1111. The sale was final. If I did not follow my instincts, my kids and I would have been homeless. I was able to survive the pandemic. My intentions were to sell and purchase a bigger home with a big yard for the kids to play. But, that did not happen at the time. I was grateful I did not have to file for bankruptcy.

I looked up the meaning of 1111. It signifies new beginnings, and you are on the right track. I never realized the significance of 1111 while living in the apartment for six years. I began to pay attention to numbers when I first had our house built. Our address, the house phone number, my cell phone number, my mother's cell phone number, and my oldest daughter's cell phone number all ended with 16. At that time, I just thought it was interesting. I was 16 when I had my oldest child. At that time, I assumed 16 had something to do with me, because my life had a major transition when I turned 16. I lost my baby brother and gained a baby girl.

The number 16 continued appearing in my life. In 2012, I was considered a high-risk pregnancy. My doctor warned me that my life and unborn child were both at risk. One of my many transitions was that I had to remove myself from an unhealthy home environment. I had to make a choice to leave for my mental and physical health, which was affecting my unborn child and children. My older children were young adults, and their friends helped us move. I drove the U-Haul truck with a huge belly. It was around Thanksgiving, so I cooked a nice meal and fed their friends. We downsized to a 2-bedroom apartment and ended in 16. I eventually leased my home to tenants.

My kids were extremely uncomfortable in a smaller space. It was heartbreaking transitioning, but finally, my son was born healthy. Unexpected circumstances occurred at the apartment. There was an emergency, and we had to relocate to another location. I can not go into details due to a legal agreement I signed not to speak on this matter in detail. I searched for another apartment and found one within the same area. I went through the new tenant process and signed the lease agreement. I noticed the unit number didn't have 16 in the address. I told my kids we lost 16. It had been our number for a while. The next day, the leasing office's manager called me to let me know another apartment was ready sooner. I went in to pick up the keys. Guess what the mailbox number was? Yes, the number 16. At that time, I had no idea what 16 meant.

I recently researched its meaning. It signifies new beginnings. The spiritual meaning is to remain positive at the moment. I was intrigued and wanted to learn more and understand more. I also realized both times, we moved from my house coincidentally around Thanksgiving.

I am eager to learn and understand more about Nikola Tesla's Theory on the numbers 3 6 9 and the magnificence of the number 9. When adding all the numbers that come before 9, the answer results with the number 9. When you add the numbers 1 through 8, it all equals 36. Then, the number 36 results in 9. The number 9 added to any number always results back to the number.

Example:

- 9 plus 1 equals 10
- Then, when you add the digits of 10, it results in 1, 9 plus 2 equals 11
- 11 results in 2, 9 plus 3 equals 12
- 12 results in 3
- You can keep adding 4, 5, 6, 7, 8, and even 9 itself.

I wanted to see what happens when multiplying 9 by each number. The final answer also results in 9.

Example:

- 9 x 1 = 9 and 9 x 2 = 18.
- Add 1 + 8 together, it results in 9
- 9 x 3 = 27. Add 2 and 7 altogether, resulting in 9.
- It continues with 9 x 4 = 36; 3 + 6 = 9, 9 x 5 = 45; 4 + 5 = 9, 9 x 6 = 63; 6 + 3 = 9
- 9 x 7 = 63; 6 + 3 = 9, 9 x 8 = 72; 7 + 2 = 9 and last but not least 9 x 9 = 81; 8 + 1 = 9

I was fascinated and interested in understanding more. I never took the time to play with numbers other than playing the lottery numbers. I began to play with the number 9 in my calculator. I have always been fascinated by the sun, moon, stars, and the vast universe. I was curious how we, as beings, are connected with the universe. Some say 9 is the universe itself.

I noticed something when I went to the movie theater the other day. I could not help but notice the seating chart had seat nine in all rows by itself. I just wonder if whoever arranged the seating chart was aware of the number nine. My curiosity made me wonder. As you know, my life changed tremendously when I turned 16. Since then, the number 16 has been connected to me from 2007 until now. I was not aware of the meaning of numbers and their synchronicities.

I summed the year 2007 as follows: 2 + 0 + 0 + 7 = 9. I started to focus on the number 16, realizing that 16 equals 7. I added 9 and 7, and it equals 16. Once again, 16! In that year, I noticed my house address, landline phone number, cell phone number, mother's cell phone number, and oldest daughter's cell number all ended in 16. At this time, I was not familiar with combining two-digit numbers into a single digit. However, the number 16 caught my attention, triggering the recollection of my baby brother's passing 3 weeks after my 16th birthday. Then, a few weeks later, I learned I was expecting my firstborn. I have been residing at my current location for 3 years now. I was under the impression that I lost the number 16 since the physical address had 4 digits, and 16 was not any of those digits. Just recently, I decided to add all 4 digits in my physical address, and the result was 16. Then, I really became curious and divided 9 by 16, which equals .5625. I added $5 + 6 + 2 + 5 = 18$; $1 + 8 = 9$. I began with the number 9, and my final result was 9.

When I was in my early twenties, my favorite 3 numbers were 777 because of my shoe size, ring size, and pant size. Besides that, I never gave much thought to numbers at that time in my life.

I remember when my Abuela would visit us from Puerto Rico. She would play games with us. One of the games involved guessing a number from 1 to 50. I think I was 5 years old at the time. For some reason, I would always just shout out 81. The adults would laugh, because it was not within the number range. They would tease me with endearment and call me 81. But now, I realized again that 8 plus 1 results in 9.

On this day, as I write, upon waking up, I dreamt of 27 multiplied by 9 was the results of 9. I looked at my phone's calculator and plugged those numbers in. The product of 27 and 9 was 243 once again added together, resulting in 9. I laid in my bed and asked God why I dreamt this. Then, a thought came in, and I decided to see if the date would be added to 9. I added 7/22/2023 altogether; the sum was 18, resulting in 9. It is my oldest granddaughter's 12th birthday.

The dream featuring the number 27 awakened a desire in me to calculate my oldest granddaughter's age, which was 12, which added up to 3. Her DOB is 7/22/2011, which adds up to 6, and the date is 7/22/2023, which adds up to 9. If you are following along, let's revisit Nikola Tesla's Theory. The final numbers are 3, 6, 9. Upon revisiting my dream involving the number 27, I experimented with the concept that any number multiplied by 9 yields 9.

The number 16 reduces to 7 in the numerology formula used to find life path's numbers. The number 7 represents wholeness and completeness. I decided to play with my birthday numbers using the digit sum method. I added up the numbers on my birthday, and it came up to 33; 3 + 3 = 6. My social security number adds up to 9. I was born on the 3rd of the month. I am the 3rd child from oldest to youngest and from youngest to oldest. My spiritual awakening began when I was 27 and added together, they equal 9.

I prayed for a better understanding of life, and slowly, things have unfolded right before my eyes. Almost everything about me that I added up in numeric form was reduced to 3, 6, and 9. Now, I am learning to understand more about the universe itself.

One night, I just could not quiet my mind. I could not sleep. I began to wonder about the time on the clock. I was once again just curious. I observed that the time on the clock is 3, 6, and 9, starting with there being 60 seconds in each minute, then 30 minutes 3 + 0 = 3, 60 minutes 6 + 0 = 6, 90 minutes 9 + 0 = 9, and 120 minutes 1 + 2 + 0 = 3. It's a 3, 6, 9 pattern.

The way we say time quarter after quarter till is 15 minutes on time. 1 + 5 = 6 quarter till is on the number 9 on the clock, which is 45 minutes; 4 + 5 = 9. The results on this were either 3, 6, or 9. Nikola Tesla said, "If you only knew the magnificence of 3, 6, 9, then you would have the key to the universe."

I recently saw a Facebook post about Toilet Tissue: "Toilet Paper Math is Harder Than Algebra." (I'm not sure who the person is who quoted this originally.) It was a collage of 6 toilet tissue brands in the USA. Of course, the comments were humorous. I, on the other hand, began adding in my head.

- The first one was Charmin Mega Tissue 9 = 36; add 3 and 6 equals 9.

- The second one was the Charmin Family Mega Tissue; 24 = 123. 24 is 2 plus 4 equals 6, and 1 plus 2 plus 3 equals 6.
- The third one was Quilted Northern Tissue 18 Mega Rolls = 72 Regular Rolls. 18 is 1 plus 8 equals 9, and 72 is 7 plus 2 equals 9.

- The fourth was Angel Soft Tissue 18 Mega Rolls = 72 Regular Rolls. 1 plus 8 equals 9, and 7 plus 2 equals 9.

- The fifth one was Charmin again, 12 Mega Rolls = 48 Regular Rolls. The number 12 is 1 plus 2 equals 3, and 48 is 4 plus 8 equals 12, which brings it to 1 plus 2 equals 3.

- The final one was Quilted Northern Ultra Plush Toilet Paper 6 Mega Rolls = 24 Regular Rolls. The number 24 is 2 plus 4 equals 6.

If I have yet to lose you, my observations are that synchronicity is everywhere; these all end in the single digits of 3, 6, and 9. Another pattern I observed involved multiplying any numbers by 3 in numerical order, consistently yielding a repetitive sequence of 3, 6, 9. Similarly, when multiplying any number by 6, a repetitive sequence of 6, 3, 9 in a different order from the 3, 6, 9 sequence. Notably, any number multiplied by 9 consistently resulted in 9. As I discovered, the results I obtained formed repetitive sequences, providing an interesting perspective on the numerical patterns and their potential connections to the universe.

During my road trip to visit my family back home, a long 12-hour ride, I ran into bumper-to-bumper traffic. We were one hour away from our destination. I started paying attention to the mile marks; there were four digits. To make time pass, I began adding the numbers in my head. Then, to entertain my children, I began to add the four digits out loud.

Each mile marker number resulted in a single-digit number. I noticed the pattern was from 1 to 9 and kept repeating itself. There was a milepost with a single digit that was consecutive with the numbers I was counting.

When I returned home, I was curious about this pattern in our number system. It was time consuming and overwhelming. It took me one week to have a breakthrough. I had to take mental breaks to understand what I was observing. You may find it as intriguing as I did or not. If so, you may need to take a break, as I did during my observations.

I randomly picked to play with 7000's and wrote the consecutive numbers down on paper. I began narrowing down this pattern, unsure if anyone in history had already figured it out. Then, I sorted numbers from 1 to 99. As the numbers went higher, I continued to use the adding digits method until the final results were a single digit. The pattern was 1 to 9. The number $99 = 9 + 9 = 18 = 9$. As I went higher, of course, the 2 digits increased, still maintaining the single-digit pattern 1 to 9. Then, I played around with 3-digit numbers, starting with $299 = 2 + 9 + 9 = 20$; $2 + 0 = 2$. My observations were that when any number ends in 9, that number is the last number in the pattern when it first results in the 2 digits after adding the digits.

The next pattern begins with any number ending in zero. The number $300 = 3 + 0 + 0 = 3$. I took 20 from the results of the number 299 ($2 + 9 + 9 = 20$) and subtracted it by 3 results of the number 300 ($3 + 0 + 0 = 3$). 20 - 3 equals 17. Then, I added $17 = 1 + 7 = 8$. The difference between this pattern is 8. I then went back to the 7000's to confirm this.

7479: 7 + 4 + 7 + 9 = 27

2 + 7 = 9

Another Example:

7480: 7 + 4 + 8 + 0 = 19

1 + 9 = 10

1 + 0 = 1

Since this number results in multiple times 19, 10, and 1, first, I subtracted 27 - 19 = 8. Then, I subtracted 27, and 10 equals 17; 1 + 7 = 8. Next, I subtracted 27 minus the 1; the results were 26; 2 + 6 = 8. I also subtracted the final single digits 9 and 1. The number 8 was the result of the difference.

Next Example:

7481: 7 + 4 + 8 + 1 =2 0

2+0=2

You can see the 1 and 2 consecutive patterns.

These patterns remain in alignment no matter the sequence. I was beyond curious about these patterns, so I decided to play with numbers ending in 99 and ending in zero. The first 3 numbers were 99, 100, and 101.

99: 9 + 9 = 18

1 + 8 = 9

100: 1 + 0 + 0 = 1

101: 1 + 0 + 1 = 2

I then subtracted 18 - 1 = 17; 1 + 7 = 8

You can see the pattern. I still wanted to see what would happen if I selected higher numbers. I chose 999 and 1000.

999: 9 + 9 + 9 = 27
2 + 7 = 9

1 + 0 + 0 + 0 = 1

I subtracted 27, and 1 equals 26 = 2 + 6 = 8. Again, 8 is the difference in this pattern when transitioning to a new pattern. Using the same adding system, I selected 3999, 4000, and 4099.

3999: 3 + 9 + 9 + 9 = 30
3 + 0 = 3

4000: 4 + 0 + 0 + 0 = 4

4099: 4 + 0 + 9 + 9 = 22
2 + 2 = 4

I continued to find the differences between when added to a single digit. The difference between the numbers 3999 and 4000, was 30 - 4 = 26; 2 + 6 = 8. Then, 3999 = 30 = 3 and 4 + 0 + 9 + 9 = 22; 2 + 2 = 4. I subtracted the 2 digit results 30 - 22 = 8, and subtracted 30 and 4 equal 26, 2 + 6 = 8. These number 8 results in the difference, and the 1 to 9 pattern continues.

I was really curious and jumped to the number 1899: 1 + 8 + 9 + 9 = 27; 2 + 7 = 9 and 1900: 1 + 9 + 0 + 0 = 10; 1 + 0 = 1. The difference between 27 and 10 is 17; 1 + 7 = 8. I took 27 minus 1. Its results were 26; 2 + 6 = 8.

Again, 8 is the difference only when the pattern is transitioning into a new pattern. The sum of two digits from a four-digit number changes its pattern consistently ending in 9s. Whenever a number ends in zero, it signifies the start of a new pattern. For example, 7525 = 19 = 10 = 1, 7526 = 20 = 2, 7527 = 21 = 3, 7528 = 22 = 4, (7529 = 23 = 5 and 7530 = 15 = 6,) 7531 = 16 = 7, the two-digit sums are not consecutive, indicating a change in pattern **(23 - 15 = 8).** However, the sum of the single digits remains consecutive, as seen with 5 and 6 and so forth.

<u>Another Example: Nnumbers Ending in 1</u>

7521 = 15 = 6,

7531 = 16 = 7

7541 = 17 = 8

This pattern 15, 16, 17 and 6, 7, 8 was another continuous on its own. All four digit numbers that end in the same digit exhibit their own consecutive patterns when their digits are summed. When grouped together such as 7521, 7531, 7541 and so forth they continue with patterns ending in 6, 7, 8 and so on. Similarly, when individual numbers are considered like 7521, 7522, 7523, the consecutive pattern continues, resulting in sequences like 6, 7, 8 and so forth.

I noticed that any number that ends with the same digit will continue a new pattern as well. These are my observations on the numbers I selected.

The final results in the pattern were always 1 to 9 repeatedly. The number zero was not in any of the single digits. It was only in the 2 digits and always followed after the number 9. When added to the single digit, it resulted in 1, beginning the 1 to 9 pattern.

At one time, zero was not considered a number. There is a long history of the number zero. It was rejected by the Western World and mostly used by the East.

The significance of the number 8 is eternity and limitless. Materialistic and spiritual. Its side resembles the symbol of infinity. Pythagoras an Ancient Greek Philosopher is best known for his contributions to mathematics particularly in the Pythagorean Theorem. He believed in the idea that numbers and mathematical relationships underlie the fundamental nature of the universe. Pythagoras also believed that the physical world was the result of combining or merging the energetic vibrations of numbers. He had established a system that corresponded letters with integers. His belief was that everything is aligned through unseen forces best expressed through numbers. Such as I have heard the universe talks to us through signs and numbers.

I know some may think this is over the top, and others may resonate with me. I'm not a mathematician, but something inside kept pushing me to figure these patterns out. I do not understand the meaning of it, but I tried to express it in the best way I can comprehend it. I am self-aware and open to learning more. I was drawn to understand the meaning of these patterned numbers. It was like a mystery to me. It's sort of like the many missing socks after washing and ending up with mix-match socks. I have yet to solve that mystery.

I appreciate life and the universe in everything. Even when I walk the Greenway, blue butterflies or dragonflies fly around me. I had two small butterflies land on my cell phone while I was trying to video them. I was fascinated at that moment. When I see a hummingbird fly and sit on my hibiscus trees, I find myself smiling. I just smile when I see living beings playing or simply just being. When I see a penny on the ground, it also makes me smile.

It is not just numbers. I believe it all plays a major part in synchronicity. I continue my self-discovery to understand the connection and meaning of numbers. I am grateful for every simple moment, thing, and all the signs the universe sends me in any form. I still do not have all the answers. Still, I have a better understanding of the meaning of numbers and how they resonated with me in synchronicity throughout my journey.

I learned to understand that during the periods of my life when I sequestered myself from others, it was God placing me in a separate place so I could be who I was meant to be. I am sure five years from now, the signs of the numbers will all make more sense to me as I continue with my journey

Proverbs 19:21 NIV

"Many are the plans in a person's heart, but it is the
LORD's purpose that prevails."

Day 

A Rising Phoenix

Autumn had arrived; the leaves covered the ground, and the trees displayed reddish-red, orange, and mustard-yellow shades. The ground was wet from the rain—nature's innate art at its best. I walked into my penthouse and placed my raincoat on the coat rack. I removed my shoes and then settled onto my sofa. I began channel surfing and started watching *House of Payne* by Tyler Perry. After a particularly lengthy day, I craved some laughter to reenergize myself.

The phone vibrated, prompting me to swipe and read the text message. It turned out to be my best friend. He asked if I would like to go out and mingle since I was single. I texted him back, "Ok, cool." He replied, "Be ready by 7 pm." Geesh. It was 5:30 pm, and my hair appeared disheveled from the rain, and I didn't have time to wash, blow dry, and straighten it.

Swiftly, I undressed and stepped into a hot shower. I applied Bath & Body Works Japanese Cherry Blossom shower gel to my sponge. I lathered my body while the hot water cascaded down my back. After rinsing, I grabbed a cotton towel from the rack to dry myself. I started massaging my favorite mango shea butter on my skin, leaving it soft as a baby's bottom. I browsed through my wardrobe, selected a burnt orange dress from the closet rack, wore my Christian Louboutin shoes, donned a long auburn wig to conceal my messy hair, grabbed my classic black Chanel purse, and spritzed on some SI by Giorgio Armani. Right on time. He texted me, "I'm here." I am grateful for these wigs. Otherwise, I wouldn't have been ready on time.

We arrived at STK on Peachtree in Atlanta. Upon entering, the hostess welcomed us with a smile and seated us at our table. Feeling famished because I skipped breakfast and lunch, I had a huge appetite. I already had a clear idea of what I wanted to eat. Our waitress approached, introduced herself, and extended her assistance. Enticed by its appealing display on the menu, I ordered the Maple Rub Ora King Salmon with pickled cherry tomatoes and piquillo broccoli with olive dressing. My friend ordered the identical meal. While waiting for our food, we relished observing the people around us.

The food was finally in front of me, and I couldn't wait to take my first bite. Its appearance and aroma were delightful, and as I indulged in a bite, it lived up to expectations. Savoring the juices and herbs of the salmon, I took a satisfying bite. The flavor was amazingly delicious. I thoroughly enjoyed and devoured my meal.

While he enjoyed his meal, I ordered a delectable cheesecake with berries and raspberries. After finishing my water, I felt so full that my belly protruded noticeably. By taking a deep breath and exhaling, I aimed to release some extra toxins, which seemed to provide relief.

I excused myself and headed to the ladies' room. As I entered the ladies' room, a couple of young ladies were thrilled, having just taken a selfie with some celebrity they ran into. As I returned to my seat, a beautiful woman with long, black, wavy hair approached me. She paused and complimented, "Love your dress and definitely that purse." I replied, "Thanks." She added, "I have one just like that."

In a surprising twist, she introduced herself, and to our coincidence, we shared the same name. Though uncommon in the U.S., it's prevalent in the Latin community. She looked at me with a smile and a twinkle in her eye as if she knew me. She seemed familiar and reminiscent of my aunties.

I sensed she was anticipating something from me, but I was unsure of what it might be. To clear the air, I just asked her, "Were you featured in Variety magazine?" Honestly, I just said the first thing that came to my mind. I couldn't place her. I have always struggled with keeping up with celebrities' names. Since the ladies earlier were so excited to take a selfie with her, she had to be someone well-known.

Before she could answer my first question about Variety magazine, I asked, "Can I get a selfie with you?" just in case she was indeed a well-known celebrity. She leaned in close and whispered in my ear, leaving me confused. I recognized her scent, Black Orchid by Tom Ford, and a hint of mango shea butter. Then she grabbed my hand. Feeling her warm hands, I still tried to process what she had whispered in my ear.

She explained to me she could not take a selfie with me because it went against the laws of the universe. She tells me, "You're becoming extraordinary. Enjoy your rose bath tonight!" Suddenly, I felt a tremble and a tug beneath my feet. "How did my Christian Louboutin disappear?" As I looked around, there was no one to be found. The ceramic tile floors vanished and turned into plain dirt. The ceiling of this edifice was opened wide. A spotlight, coming from the sky, was beaming down on me. The walls came tumbling down into thin air. There I was, standing in the middle of a forest.

I couldn't move my feet. I was rooted to the ground. The light became brighter. I could feel the heat sensation. I began to let go. Suddenly, I felt lighter, as if I was floating. I felt free, letting go of my fears, worries, and burdens. The light permeated through my veins, organs, and entire body. My heart was full of overflowing love and joy.

I felt something loose inside my head, releasing my mind. The light was so bright, showering all around me. I was feeling blissful. I then realized that the woman who stopped me was me. No wonder she seemed so familiar. She had the same black classic Chanel bag. It was my 40th birthday gift. Her scent was my favorite perfume.

It all made sense when she whispered in my ear. It happened so fast. As I recalled her words, "Enjoy your rose bath tonight", no one knew about my rose baths. I began to process it all, she was a better version of myself.

Taking a deep breath, exhaling, and smiling, I looked around.

Then, my alarm sounds. I woke up feeling rejuvenated and ready to co-create my life story. I thanked the universe for everything. I reflected on my past experiences for just a visit to see how far I had come. I had to face and embrace all of myself to become better.

Growing up, I experienced racism within and outside of my race. Though I believe our outer appearances should not matter, we are all one race, the human race, and our true selves are from the same source. I am of Puerto Rican descent. As a young girl, I was disappointed with my mom for marrying my dad because I had his physical appearance. My dad is Afro-Latino brown-skinned with coarse hair. My hair is naturally curly. Without hair products, it's frizzy. My mom did not have the knowledge or money to buy products to enhance my natural curls.

My skin tone was either too dark or too light yellow-toned, depending on who I was around. There were always negative comments about my skin color during the summer because I would tan dark. The other Puerto Rican kids would tell me I looked like a black girl, as if it was a bad thing. Upon high school graduation, an old Puerto Rican friend commented that I was attractive if I was a black girl. At that time, I did not know how to respond, but now I recognize it was an inappropriate remark. I used to daydream about looking as beautiful as a model someday. I felt dissatisfied with my skin tone. I longed for acceptance just as I was. This was mainly my experience growing up in my Latin community. I was the oddball and never understood how skin color was considered beauty.

While the skin serves as the body's largest organ, the key to love and acceptance shouldn't hinge on its color; rather, the focus should be on maintaining skin health. Inner beauty radiates the outer beauty, enhancing the true beauty of others, irrespective of their skin tone.

I have witnessed it even as an adult. An acquaintance of mine, who was Mexican, invited me to an event. My baby girl, who was seven years old, came back to me crying. The other kids told her she could not play with them because she was black. I was furious. I told my acquaintance what happened, and we left.

There was another incident with my children, who were older at the time. They attended a Hispanic event, and the host asked her sister to serve the children. Her sister, who was lacking awareness, claimed not to know what black people ate. My children understood and shared the experience with me. Once again, it affected me because these were my children who were hurt. I felt disheartened as now my children had to encounter racism as well. If only I could travel back in time to discover the origins of this prejudice based on skin color and perhaps influence a change in perspective.

That same old acquaintance's best friend was Mexican as well. She asked me to lease my house to them. But, her only specifications were as long as she would not have black neighbors. My response to her was, "What? My family was black." Her reaction was as if she was confused. I distanced myself from them. A few years later, I saw them buddy-buddy with another associate, who was African American. The hypocrisy made my blood boil. During this time, I was in a dark place. I was not aware how to process it all.

I have also encountered individuals from other races expressing their discomfort through racial remarks. I would strive to be in diverse environments. I despise racism in every form. I always witness it both ways because of my skin tone and ethnicity.

I severed ties with individuals holding such a mindset. Embracing my olive complexion despite facing prejudice from individuals of different races, including mine. Every race opposite me, especially my race. With time, I understand not everyone has this same mindset, only the ones lacking awareness. This is based on my experience.

In another aspect of my upbringing, a noteworthy detail is that I had a cousin whom my mom's older brother adopted. His wife's sister was brown-skinned, and her husband was fair-skinned. Both were Puerto Rican. Their first daughter was born fair-skinned, and the second daughter was brown-skinned. The father loved his wife with brown skin but didn't want a baby with brown skin. So, they gave the brown-skinned daughter to the mother's sister. She was raised as a niece and cousin to her blood sister. My parents told us the truth, or maybe I overheard them talking. I was aware of this at an early age, and we had to keep it a secret.

Breaking the Cycle

I was so naive and gullible because I grew up with low self-esteem and a lack of confidence and awareness. As I got older, I experienced infidelity and unhealthy relationships for almost two decades. I was stuck in a low vibrational place. Despite everything, I didn't let anything bring me down completely.

Once upon a time, I always thought something was wrong with me. I never found my place in peer groups and became a loner. I often went places alone and found enjoyment in my own company. That is where my observation of people began.

I continued to observe people wearing so many masks, pretending to like someone when they despised them for their outer appearances. It goes back to holding resentment from the past that has been passed down in their DNA. The hatred, anger, frustrations, and so on. These people never took the time to heal, forgive, accept, and love unconditionally, regardless of their outer appearance. This was being passed down generations. The future generations of tomorrow are still holding on to resentment and hatred. Will there be a time when racism no longer exists? That's my question. Will all mankind come to an awareness that we are here to love?

Despite experiencing disappointments, loss, and pain, I resiliently rose again and guided by my innate wisdom, I recognized I deserved better. I summoned the courage to take the steps necessary for self-improvement. I released everything that did not serve me any purpose. If it felt heavy in my spirit, it had to go. I had to separate myself from old limited beliefs, to learn to protect my energy, and begin to have to be a better version of myself for me.

I took the time to process, heal, forgive, let go, and love. I have remained single for over ten years. I did not want to enter a new relationship with baggage from my past. I was like a bird in a cage with the door open, not realizing I could fly and set myself free. I only saw myself inside a cage. When I realized the door was always open, I spread my wings and flew far away from the cage.

I was exhausted at the way I allowed others to mistreat me. So, I changed my reactions to others' behaviors. I worked on where I placed my energy. I focused on my inner being and protecting my energy from those who did not have good intentions toward me. I understood I was exuding low self-esteem that attracted low vibrational beings.

I understand I am an empath and absorb others' energy. I have been working on protecting my energy and space from what does not serve me any purpose. I felt empowered when I finally set myself free. I began to comprehend how not to judge others, though I may not like their behavior towards me. We are not supposed to judge. We are spiritual beings inside a human body, and the human part of us will judge others.

I began praying for those who still living from a place of hurt to find their inner peace and heal. We are all co-creators and can choose to be our own directors in our life stories. It almost seems that there were only two scripts to choose from. Just as that saying goes, "SAME SCRIPT, DIFFERENT CAST." I chose a new script full of gratitude and abundance. Saying affirmations and confirmations became a new habitual behavior.

Many people cross paths and realize they have similar experiences. I know I have met many women, even men, who have had experiences similar to mine. We have naturally chosen these scripts since childhood, sponging everything we saw, heard, and experienced. Our experiences and life paths have led us to connect in one way or another to impact someone's life for the better. Even if it was a terrible situation, one learns from it and knows what they would tolerate and what they truly desire and deserve.

Every one of us deserves love and happiness. We have to do the work going within. Focusing on our inner world is what I have learned along the way through my triumph. I thank every individual who has impacted me negatively or positively.

Our subconscious mind is like a program on a hard drive in a computer. We have the will to choose a script from a scarcity mindset with complacency, pain, struggles, and disappointments in relationships, finances, and careers, or choose the I know who I am born from love with birthrights, infinite abundance, love, success, health, prosperity, and freedom.

I began to embrace myself as the being I was and accepted my body inside and out. I wanted to know who I was besides what I knew. I took a DNA test and learned I am one-third Iberian (Spain/Sardinia) and African (Egyptian, Moroccan, Libya, Sierra Leone, and majority Nigerian). Central America did not have highlighted areas, just the entire region in this part of the world. I began soul searching. I appreciated my ancestors' DNA. This is why I have never fit in. I was not created to fit in; I am designed this way for a reason.

Everything was beginning to make sense to me. I did ask for a better understanding of life in my prayers. I was abusing my body from overbinging on toxic foods to negative thoughts. I began to tell the difference when my energy felt heavy. I chose to make that change. It is a lighter and more peaceful feeling. Every day, I receive a sign from the universe directing me or reminding me to stay on track. I do not have any regrets.

It was Labor Day weekend, and my ten year old son and I were walking the greenway with my youngest daughter's mixed Yorkie dog. He reminds me of Scrappy Doo from Scooby Doo. There was a couple, a Caucasian man and an Asian lady, both walking two Pit Bulls. The White Pit Bull charged to attack my daughter's Yorkie mix. His muzzle was loose because the owners loosened it during their run in the greenway. The owner lost grip on him, and he charged towards us. My son was on his rollerblades holding our dog's leash. My first response was to get our dog from the ground to protect him from this aggressive white Pit Bull trying to harm him. I could not bear the thought of watching another life get hurt in front of me, especially my daughter's dog.

My son was holding him, and when I saw the white Pit Bull charging towards them, I impulsively grabbed him by the leash in the air, trying to keep him far from this aggressive Pit Bull. The Pit Bull jumped on me and knocked me down on the concrete, hurting my head. I lost hold of our dog's leash. I was flat on my back on the ground, thinking he harmed him. I asked God what was the lesson behind this unfortunate traumatizing event. I replayed it over and over in my head and kept thinking it could have been worse. If I had told my son to run off carrying our dog on his blades, the Pit Bull would have chased them. I would have been devastated for making a poor judgment call. I was relieved we remained there, and my son was not the one getting hurt during this awful incident. Back to the incident, the owner finally got a grip on his Pit Bull's muzzle leash. They apologized and said they got the dog from a shelter six months ago.

I went to the emergency room. I was so disappointed to see my blood pressure elevating to 160/107 since I had done the work for over one year with no medications. When I got home, our dog cuddled under me as if he knew I risked myself to protect him from harm. My son said he no longer wanted to go back to the greenway. Walking the greenway was the highlight of my everyday routine.

I was pleased later that week when I went to my Doctor for a follow-up. My blood pressure was 128/80, and my side effects were tailbone discomfort. But I was determined to reverse it back to its original state. It felt good to hear my doctor acknowledge the mind management work I had practiced daily to remain off medications. I continued to pay attention to my breathing, listen to healing frequencies, practice mind management, and read my confirmations and affirmations.

Yes, I endured the emotional stress, physical pain, and more medical bills added to my plate with barely a consistent income flow. A few weeks went by, and the owners of the dog went back on their word and refused to pay my medical bills. I was disappointed in myself because I trusted them and protected them. I did not report their dog at that time. My son told me he didn't trust them that day, but didn't dare say anything because he knew I would think they were genuine as I did. I couldn't believe people could be so cold-hearted and irresponsible.

After almost two months, my son and I finally returned to the greenway. Our first time doing this, we charged some water on the full moon and poured it back to the earth. I felt at peace again connecting with nature. My son remembered exactly where it took place. I couldn't remember much of it as he did. As he described the incident, it was heartbreaking that he experienced that pain. I became extremely skittish of dogs walking by. We walked with large, thick sticks as tall as we were for protection. And we faced the fear.

Two weeks later, it was sunny in the mid-afternoon. I was walking back to my car alone on the phone with my youngest daughter from the greenway. I saw two Pit Bulls on the trail on my right side. I instantaneously stopped holding my stick on the ground to let them go by. I felt like a shepherd waiting for my flock to catch up. I noticed the white Pit Bull was the one that charged me. The feeling was so awkward. I remained calm. Thankfully, I was still on the phone with my baby.

Since the day of the incident was so overwhelming, I didn't realize what the other Pitt Bull looked like in detail. Its face was white, and its body was brown. The male owner was alone with both, and he recognized me. We locked eyes, and he turned away from me headed back towards the trail. Once again, I didn't understand his reaction when his dog hurt me and my son's emotional pain. I remained grateful and did not lose my faith.

I returned home, looked in the mirror, and asked God why this happened. What was my lesson to learn? I still had these medical bills. I had to let it go and let God handle the uncomfortable things happening. I understood I had to go through all the unwanted and wanted things to be here today, sharing my story. I learned to forgive and love myself unconditionally to know who I am. I had to unlearn the old program and relearn a new program. It's similar to wiping out a cell phone with too much storage.

I had heard life is a game. There are simple rules to play this game. Be self-aware of your thoughts and be careful of what you ask for. Be mindful and wish good on others as you wish for yourself. Be kind, spread love, and the universe will, in return, give back to you what you asked for. My choices in coping with my past experiences define who I am becoming.

My soul absorbs every moment and experience. My ego tries to protect me from a place of fear in survival mode since that is its purpose: doing anything to protect me. I had to learn how to stand up to my ego. I wanted a different change in my life. I chose to change my old ways of living and choose a better way to live in the present moment.

When I decided to no longer be a hostage to the ego and allowed myself to become a host to the divine, I released all the old limited beliefs. Then, I started contemplating life's challenges, envisioning obstacles like a Crow attacking an Eagle. The Crow lands on the Eagle and bites the Eagle. Yet, the Eagle will ignore the Crow. The Crow gets a free short ride until the Eagle elevates higher. The higher it rises, the Crow will fall because it needs oxygen.

I realized I could not continue down the same old path. I had to elevate and maintain momentum and stop giving the challenges and obstacles a free ride. I began to lead the dance, no longer the ego in the lead. The Spirit of God resides within me, a pure consciousness of love. I am one with God.

2 Corinthians 3:16-18

"Nevertheless when it shall turn to the Lord, the vail shall be taken away. Now the Lord is that Spirit: and where the Spirit of the Lord is, there is liberty. But we all, with open face beholding as in a glass the glory of the Lord, are changed into the same image from glory to glory, even as by the Spirit of the Lord."

Day 

The Mightiness of Manifestations

As I reminisce about my past, I realize that I manifested a lot of unforeseen situations in my life. I was not aware that I was manifesting as a young girl. I was extremely shy and soft-spoken. When I was nine years old, every girl in the church had a tambourine. I wanted one so badly. My dad traveled to Puerto Rico for my cousin's funeral. May he rest in peace. I wrote on a piece of paper, "Please tell my Papi to buy me a tambourine and placed it in the heater vent. When my dad returned to the States, he opened up his suitcase, and there was a small tambourine just for me. As an adult, I asked my mom if she found the note in the vent, and she said she did not. I unwillingly used my innate power. I imagined my dad buying the tambourine for me. I was manifesting without being taught to do so.

Some of my classmates and peers were pregnant in the ninth grade. A few of them would give their babies up for adoption and continue their education. I was nosy and always asked them if they were still with the father. Some would respond with "Yes." I never thought I would be a statistic single teen mom. Somehow, I manifested it unknowingly to be a single mother.

I witnessed seeing friends manifesting their lives, and it unfolded. We are all powerful manifesters whether we are aware of it or not. Our thoughts hold so much power, especially when you marry them with your emotional feelings. Unifying the mind and heart creates your thoughts into reality, and everything you desire comes to fruition in due time. Sometimes, when you least expect it.

I have learned that every lesson is a blessing, and there is a reason why some people are in your life for a season. I am sure if you look back at your life, you will realize you have claimed an event or circumstance that has taken place in your life, all because you attached a feeling to it innately. Let's say you were invited somewhere, and you do not really want to go, but you do not want to hurt someone's feelings. Coincidentally, the event was canceled. Just any random thought that comes to your mind, then you say I knew that was going to happen.

We are so distracted we can not sit and quiet our minds for five minutes to give it a break. We are all powerful beings. I am sure if everyone focused on love and becoming a better version of themselves, the world would be a better place for future generations to come. We have lost our true connection to the universe, being programmed to operate in fear.

As a little girl, I experienced the fear of being outcasted. As I got older, I experienced racism within and outside my ethnicity. As an adult, I witnessed racism and prejudice in many forms, depending on the crowd. It also came from a place of pain and suffering early on. I was conformed to believe everything about me was wrong, bad, or ugly. If it was not that my skin color was considered yellow-toned or too dark, it was my body for naturally being born with a buttock, my natural frizzy, curly hair, walking pigeon-toed, and much more.

I never fit in anywhere. I became a loner, and as an adult, I still am, and I am happy. I can travel alone, go out to an event, dinner, or movies alone, and enjoy myself. I was always the last to be chosen for teams during my school years. But now, I understand I had to experience all of it to become me.

Now, I realize that I allowed myself to entertain unhealthy relationships. I was the only one in my immediate family with children out of wedlock. Sitting back and reflecting on my story, I had no reason to be ashamed. Society created an image and expectations of perfection or what they had in place. Going way back to ancient times, it has always existed. It was a time when only boys were allowed to train to become scribes. There has always been some form of box to fit in.

If one person did not look or behave like the majority, they were an outcast. The fact that, at one time, left-handers were not accepted in a right-handed world is crazy to me. Especially being born a lefty and now ambidextrous due to conformity. Was I angry with God, my family, the church, or society as a whole? Of course not. Deep down, I was angry with myself for directing my energy in the wrong direction, but I had to release that fire burning from deep within in order to comprehend that everything was aligned to take place the way it had already been played out to be for me to fully transform and become a beacon of light in this world.

I now know that being a single mother is nothing to be ashamed of. My fraternal great-grandmother and maternal grandmother were single mothers, and they did their best as single mothers. I have raised four children, who are 31, 30, 23, and 11 years old. I always felt alone, but I was never alone. Just as I wanted something different for my children, my older children chose to get married at an early age.

I stopped worrying about what others thought about me. I removed my veils and began living in the present moment. I stopped pleasing others when I felt uncomfortable. I stopped playing small so others could feel better. I no longer was emitting the lack of and attracting the lack of. When I noticed discomfort, I became self-aware of my breathing and placed my hand over my heart. I took deep breaths and exhaled, and within no time, I could feel at ease.

I am trusting my path and embracing the good and the difficulties. I know everything that is happening is working out for me; this was not happening to me but for me. I am no longer a victim in my circumstances nor a slave in my own body. I surrendered to the freedom of joy.

As my life unfolded, though there were many challenges, I began to grow wiser and more resourceful. I taught my children dignity, morals, and values. I was able to enjoy being a mother and have fun with my friends. My children were loved. I wanted to live a different life than the one my parents gave me. I moved my children to the suburbs and took them on vacations when I could. I grew up with my children.

After experiencing a hurricane while living in Florida, I learned to detach from materialistic things. I kept birthdays intimate and simple. I also cut back on Christmas overspending. As long as I cooked them their favorite meals with some TLC, they were happy with my new normal. It was a priceless time and full of love.

As a young mother, I tried my best to raise my children and aimed to be the best I could be. I did not have the instructions to be a single mother. However, I connected with great people, and some pointed me in the right direction. I had to learn as time went by. I learned that my only competition was myself from yesterday. I consciously chose to heal my heart and mind to free my soul. I did not allow my past pain to prevent me from becoming who I was becoming. Though nothing ever stays on the same course. I learned that everything that has happened in my life was not to me, but for me to become the woman I am.

As I continued with my self-discovery of my relationship with God, the One Creator source of all living beings, I became wiser and stronger. I realize now that I have been connected with nature since I was a child, playing outside and climbing trees, even as I wrote my thoughts, desires, and wishes on paper. I know that God resides within me.

I always knew what I wanted since I was a child. I was just afraid to let go of what I was accustomed to. I was afraid to take risks of the unknown. I had one foot in and one foot out. I was brave when I entered this world from my mother's womb; my innate wisdom was to take my first breath. Then, fear was programmed into my mind, which turned into conformity. I had to face many adversities to learn to be brave once again. I took a leap of faith with both feet. I then began to have clarity of my true purpose in this world. I jumped in with a blindfold, and now I feel peace within. I am here for a purpose.

Becoming a mother at an early age and overcoming all the trials and tribulations I experienced, I can share my story. It's a gift in itself. I do not regret any of my experiences. I learned a lesson from each one of them. Sometimes, I was redirected by the Divine to get me on the right path to level up and stop taking my life for granted. If I were asked to change something from my past, I would say I would listen to my intuition. I am who I am today because of my past and each experience.

For a long time, my prayers at night consisted of asking God to give me strength and remove those he knew had bad intentions toward me. They were removed slowly but surely from my life. I was never good at discerning. I thought everyone that smiled with me was my friend. I stepped aside and let God clean my space for me. I felt better having a better understanding of everything around me. Now, I fully comprehend, I got what I asked for.

I needed circumstances to take place so that I could gain strength. I asked God to reveal the truth when I was in an unhealthy situation. I received signs that led me to the truth. I realized deep down there was something about me, but I did not know how to tap into it to see. I just kept reflecting on moments in my life when I said I wanted something or just daydreaming about it, and it came true. A few people might resonate with me in many ways. We all have this innate wisdom inside of us.

Every time I was expecting one of my children, I would pray every night for a healthy girl or boy, depending on my desire for each pregnancy. My prayers were answered. I always thanked God for my blessings.

As I continued to keep my conversations in my mind consistent, I was mastering the understanding of reversing "Why did this happen to me?" to "This happened for me!" I became self-aware of my fears and thoughts and found inner peace. I began to pay attention to how I was feeling when I was having certain conversations. I recognized when it was time to move my energy.

I intend to share my story to inspire young single mothers or anyone who will resonate with me. Yes, you can fulfill your dreams. You can do anything you set your mind to do. Journaling is a great way to manifest what you want to accomplish. I have written down my thoughts, feelings, and experiences since I was young. A habitual behavior I am glad I absorbed and continuing. Anyone can because we all have a mind, not just a mind, but a powerful one; we can choose to control. Practice self-discipline and train it to work for oneself.

As we all are in self-discovery, we should surround ourselves with like-minded individuals—those who are inspiring and willing to share their successes. We innately attract what we are feeling inside. It first begins with a thought that is a vibration that leads to an emotion. Each of us has a chalice waiting for us to keep it overflowing with abundance. Abundance can be anything you desire: freedom, peace, happiness, health, love, money, and more.

When you ask for what your heart desires, you will receive it. It may not be on your time, but you will receive it. Everyone has access to this. There is enough abundance to go around. Focus on the feeling, how you would feel when you receive it. Always assume that you are already living it in the present moment.

As I trained as an actor and continued to observe my mind and body, it helped me understand the concept of it all. When you fail, get back up and strive even harder the next time. For every failure or rejection, it is a success to the next step—no stands for the next opportunity. When we were toddlers, innately, we got back up when we fell. We are born with resilience. We had a deep knowledge, but somewhere along the lines, we forgot as we evolved due to our surroundings and environment.

Other living species understand their purpose without guidance; they follow their natural instinct. When a baby giraffe is born, they must learn to walk within one hour of being in the new world. I am amazed by all living beings and their way of being. Each of them are aligned with the one Creator, and so are we.

My youngest son was confused about God, the Creator of all. He said he didn't see him. I had to explain to him the process of breathing air. We can not see air, but it's everywhere, and we rely on it to live. We can survive without water or food for a few days or so, but we can not survive without oxygen in the air. I said to him God is everywhere. He lives within every-thing he created. I expressed to him the vastness of the water in the ocean and that every living being has water inside their body and needs water to live.

I had to become an example and let him observe me in hopes that he would apply these tools in his life. We were created to love. It is the purest feeling to experience coming from the heart's space. After all, the heart is the first organ developed in the fetus.

We do not have excuses to remain complacent. Do not choose to be dormant; do it for yourself and your descendants. We are here to live an abundant life full of love to serve others with love and compassion. As I continue my journey, I understand I am here to learn as I go, share knowl-edge, and serve purposefully.

Proverbs 20:5

"Counsel in the heart of man is like deep water; but a man of understanding will draw it out."

Acknowledgment

I thank my parents for always supporting my passions and dreams.

I want to thank Flora Reynolds, my grandmother, for her unconditional love.

To my mentor, Javon Johnson, for pushing me to set the intention to write my book and complete the process.

To Vickie Adams for always believing in me.

To my coach Mike Pointer for encouraging me to share my story with the world.

I give special thanks to my daughter-in-law, Katherine, and son-in-law, Coite.

Thank you, Dr. Nyisha D. Davis (The Book Birthing Midwife), for her guidance and support.

Thank you to every person I have come in contact with in any way and who played a role in my life, which led me to find the courage to share my story. I am grateful to all!

1 John 3:1 (NIV)
"See what great love the Father has lavished on us, that we should be called children of God! And that is what we are! The reason the world does not know us is that it did not know him."

Nereida Velazquez

Reference

Meditativemind.org. (2023). Nicola Tesla's 3-6-9 Theory: What You Need
     To Know. Retrieved from https://meditativemind.org/nicola-teslas-
     3-6-9-theory-what-you-need-to-know%EF%BF%BC/#:~:text
     =The%20secret%20of%20the%20universe&text=In%20a%20
     1931%20interview%2C%20Tesla,the%20universe%20and%20
     its%20mysteries.

Plato.standford.edu. (2024). Stanford Encyclopedia of Philosophy
     Retrieved from https://plato.stanford.edu/entries/pythagoras/

www.ingramcontent.com/pod-product-compliance
Lightning Source LLC
Chambersburg PA
CBHW050344160726
48002CB00001B/447